The Georgian Rose Press
georgianrose@eircom.net

First published 2008

Second Edition 2008

© 2008 by Jo Wardhaugh Doyle

The moral right of the author has been asserted.

ISBN 978-0-9534167-3-8

In Memory
to the Ugandan Man Whose Name I Never Knew.

"When you looked at me
Your eyes imprinted your grace in me;
For this you loved me ardently;
And thus my eyes deserved
To adore what they beheld in you."
(Stanza 32. The spiritual Canticle.)

In Thanksgiving For
Mum and Dad,
Frances and Clare,
Maud,
Claire,
Jim,
Jackie,
Ed,
Dave,
Robin,
Kathleen
Lissa
and lastly for my beloved Matthew.

YOUTH

I had a very normal child hood growing up in a happy place in Edinburgh or so I thought. It was only when I was older that I realised that my father was a very famous Edinburgh footballer known as "twinkle toes". He was part of the Terrible Trio of Conn, Bauld and Wardhaugh who took The Scottish League by storm in the 1950s. He played for The Heart of Midlothian football club and Scotland, and was known as gentleman Jim because he was never booked in all the games he played. Many well known footballers of today will still talk with admiration about his skills and character. Sir Alex Ferguson himself was known to admire my father and look up to him, wanting to emulate his boyhood hero.

My mother, too, was a great sportswoman at school in Edinburgh. So it was no wonder that we all became good at sports, becoming captains of our netball teams, hockey and volleyball teams. Indeed, my eldest sister, Frances, played hockey for Scotland and to this day is a keen and committed sportswoman. I would not be able to count how many marathons, half marathons, 10kms and triathlons she has done. My other sister, Clare, and she enjoy a 10km jog and triathlon together. One day I may do a leg of a triathlon with them, but as yet there is not a chance.

Much of our childhood grew up with memories of sport, holidays in Gullane (a smashing beach outside Edinburgh) and Cornwall and Devon. We all became expert body board surfers and loved the outdoor life. The three of us girls joined the Edinburgh Southern Harriers Athletic Club and we whiled away our teenage years having great and exciting fun.

One of my great moments was when I was 15 years old and was entered into the British Games. I was a shot putter and threw that day against Mary Peters and Rosemary Payne. I was 7th and was excited that maybe in a few years time I might qualify for the Commonwealth Games.

It was all about that time that I realised that we were a well known family in Edinburgh because of my father. Every time one of us ran, threw or jumped our names were in the papers, usually saying something like, "Today, Jimmy Wardhaugh's daughter was third in the Scottish Games", etc. We never really had to be first to get a mention!

We were brought up in a Catholic home but it wasn't all prayers and rosaries, it was more like look out for the less fortunate and if there is someone lonely then stay a while with them. Indeed, our school upbringing mirrored our home upbringing. Every Friday afternoon was a time for a different type of education and when we reached 4th and 5th years we were allowed to visit the elderly around the school. This was part of our curriculum and was set up by the school. We all had people to visit and usually I would clean windows, do some small shopping and then have a cup of tea and a chat.

We had opportunities to do other things, too, on a Friday afternoon, like going to Hillend were the artificial ski slope was, or do some creative art. When I think of it we were a lucky generation, we had freedom, trust and small responsibilities.

I had loved primary school but never particularly had that warm happy feel about school once I left junior education. Secondary school was ok and I had many friends and was reasonably popular. I was very, very strong too, being a shot putter, and we would race each other to 20 one-armed press-ups, which I frequently won.

At school I loathed and could not tolerate bullies. I remember seeing one gentle boy being shoved and pushed and kicked by three or four brats. I went in and clobbered them, spreading them in all directions. I moved away quickly from the bullied lad as I did not want to embarrass him about being saved by a girl. Another time when I was at school there was a lad in the corridor behind me. He kept tripping me up and standing on my heel. I turned and asked him not to do that again. He was a good 4 inches taller than I and he smirked and tripped me up again. I turned at the speed of lightening, grabbed his neck collar, lifted him off his feet and crashed him against the corridor wall. I told him to back off. I was so strong and he was a light weight. At that moment a teacher passed and looked at the scenario, nodded and said, "I see you have the situation in hand Joanne!" I put the bully down and let him scuttle away feeling humiliated and ashamed.

We were a strong family and my father became our physiotherapist when we hurt ourselves, which we did frequently. He had a few sayings like, "Now for the Hot and COLD treatment", which was for any strain or sprain. Ice cubes and hot, hot water alternatively did the trick for most things. "Walk through the pain" was another, and "It's as simple as that" was the most famous. My mother at times reminded Dad that we were little girls not footballers, but most of the time we laughed and trusted Dad's remedies, because they worked.

One time I had been playing hockey on the all weather pitch and fell full force at high speed. I literally burned the skin off my leg, but like a good Wardhaugh "played through the pain". I walked home pulling my socks up to my knees so no one would see. The next morning I couldn't put my leg to the ground. It was inflamed and dirty, even though I had washed it down with water. The pain was bad. Dad popped me up on the dining room table and looked at it. He thought a good dose of peroxide would clean it all up and right enough when the peroxide was being poured on the leg it all fizzed up white and bubbly. The next thing I knew was that I was being held up by my arm pits by Mum and Dad with my head out the window. I lay down, felt better, had my breakfast and walked to school, as Dad said, "Walk through the pain, and don't let it tighten up." Right enough I was grand by the next day.

I have lots of memories, one being when I fell sick and needed to be hospitalised for 2 weeks. I had had the 'flu' then got another attack of it; I ended up run down and quite unwell and was unable to eat and barely drink properly. These 2 weeks wore me out, but at the same time I watched the nurses and thought they were great. I had wanted to be a gym teacher up till then, but now I knew I wanted to be a nurse.

After being hospitalised I never regained my level of fitness, but continued to play hockey and volleyball. When I reached 5th year I had enough qualifications to leave school and become a nurse. I trained at the Royal Infirmary of Edinburgh. I loved nursing. I felt I had come home to myself. It was not like work. Some of the old ward sisters were of the old stalk and could absolutely terrify and intimidate, but there was not one of them that I did not learn good nursing practice from. The patients were well cared for and we certainly knew every detail about them and their condition. We were all encouraged to get the Nursing Mirror, which we did, as we were hungry to learn more and more about nursing. None of that was a chore and like any good nurse in training we had a wild social and night life. We had boundless energy and if we were tired after a shift, then we went out and reenergized. Our food was partying, holidays, fellas and fun. The telly at that time was The Liver Birds, Angels, Starsky And Hutch and Mash.

After the first year in the nurses' home, which contrary to what it sounds like was "ab fab" fun, three of us moved into a one bed-roomed flat. It was brilliant. Our first taste of really being grown up and it was mental. That lasted for about a year and then five of us moved into a flat closer to the hospital. When I look back on these times we must have been a nightmare for the neighbours and they must have loved it when we went onto night duty. We usually did 8 week blocks of 8 nights on 2 off, then 7 nights on 4 off. We didn't mind and our nights off were lived to the full.

Much of the carry on was harmless growing up. We all had boyfriends which lasted anything from 2 weeks to a year. Our hearts were broken and then in love, what a roller coaster of a journey, but great fun and we all loved nursing and were good at it.

Then five months before my nursing finals, my dad dropped dead. Shock does not come close to what we all felt. He was fit, not overweight and did not smoke or drink. It was January 2nd 1978, Dad went to report on a new year football match, but he never made it home. He got off the club's bus and was walking home when he dropped dead. Seemingly some people passed him by as they thought he was drunk. Then one man saw that the man lying in the street was well dressed and was not drunk but dying. He was 48 years old and was dead by the time the ambulance came.

Numb, yet in severe pain with a terrible loss. It hurt me so much that people had walked over him and I vowed that I would never do that to anyone. Indeed even as an 8 year old kid I had seen someone falling all over the place at a bus stop, a number of the adults were ignoring this woman, but I did not. I went to a shop and asked them to phone an ambulance. The ambulance came and it was found out that the woman was a diabetic. I did not at that age understand why a diabetic would fall around the place but I did know that I helped that woman and I was only 8.

I moved back home. All the wild stuff seemed empty and pointless now. I was lost and devastated, but had a very nice boyfriend during that time who was very kind and patient. Loss like that brings on extreme pain which deepens you. I saw patients and their relatives' losses in a deeper way. Even though I was still only 20, I felt I could stand with them better in their sorrow

I became more reflective and introspective during that year, asking serious questions about the meaning of life and the meaning of love. All I knew is that I loved Dad and now he was gone and what was it all about. My 21st birthday came with no Dad. My mum was great, though, and we had a party and a special meal at a hotel where we always used to go for special family occasions. My mum was only 46, my brother 12 and we three girls all in our early 20s: Dad was missed beyond reason.

I was now a qualified nurse and was working in a female medical ward specialising in liver disease. I always thought the patients in that ward were special, they were so ill and very frightened. One time I had just come back after being in Shetland for Uphellia, the Viking festival, which may I say is an experience in a life time, I came back to start my 8 week stint of night duty. To my shock, there was a girl from my school in my ward extremely ill. I could not believe it, someone my age and dying. She was always a lovely person at school but angelic in illness. She touched my hurting soul even more, it was all too unbelievable why someone my age, but so good and beautiful, could be dying. I owned a motorbike and every morning coming off duty I would ride to mass before going home. I prayed. I did not know how to pray properly (if there is a proper way) so I took my dad's Sunday Missal and asked God to let her live. This went on every day, as I realised with every night she was getting sicker. I bargained with God that I would do something worthwhile with my life if she lived.

She died March 1979 and I was saddened into not being able to feel anything. I was numb, shocked and unable to find any taste in partying and fooling around. Even though she had died, I said to God that I would still "do something" with my life. What, I did not know yet.

I had always as a child been attracted to heroic figures. I was of a generation born only 12 years after the end of WW2. We were influenced by the Great Escape, Colditz and The Wooden Horse stories. Films like Odette and Carve Her Name With Pride were always on telly; yet another film which had a massive impact on me was the story of Gladys Aylward in the Inn of the Sixth Happiness. She was a missionary heroine in war torn China, she saved children and was brave. I wanted to do something with my life more than just partying, so I thought maybe for a few years I could go abroad and help! As a youngster Borneo had always attracted me, as had Peru, but I couldn't find any groups going there. Indeed my Nana nearly had apoplexy when getting the wrong end of the stick thinking I was going to go to Borneo on my motor bike! I assured her that that would not happen…yet…any how.

I looked around for a lay missionary group to go to the Third World. I found the VMM, Volunteer Missionary Movement, and went to London and did a 2 month preparation course. There was an Irish girl called Catherine Horan whom I became quite friendly with. She too wanted to do something with her life for a year or two and as the preparatory course progressed we found out that she was flying out to Ortum in Kenya and I was being sent to Gulu in Uganda. I remember asking not to go to a violent place and I was not keen on teaching, although I had done and quite enjoyed clinical teaching of the students on the ward. I was told that Idi Amin had been ousted out of the country and I in my utter naivety presumed that if he had just left, then all would be fine. I said yes to that assignment. I was filled with excitement and hope, but a wrenching sadness at leaving my mum. She had supported me all the way and was not going to let her grief hold me back.

Catherine and I flew out together on 31st March 1980. Catherine was worried about her brother, whose wife was having their first baby, and I sadly said a fond farewell to my whole family. I promised my Nana I would not be riding a motor bike in Africa! Little did I know.

This was the end of my naivety, this was the end of my childhood.

UGANDA

Our first encounter with the "outside" world was when we stopped late at night in Egypt. To this day I do not know what airline we flew out with, but I am sure that we were not meant to stop in Cairo. There had been really bad thunder and lightening storms on the journey and I do remember people being violently sick.

Well here we were in Cairo, 22 years old and beginning to think "What have I let myself in for?" Our passports were gathered from us and taken away, both Catherine and Steve had to hand over cigarettes, too. We all huddled together and were not told about our ongoing flight, there was no information whatsoever. It was a dingy corner we were put into and we seemed to be the only Europeans around. I felt very alone and frightened with no passport. After just 4 hours or so, smoking our brains out, there was a man who told us all to step out on to the run way and find our suitcases. All of a sudden we were on the run way scrambling to point out our cases. I wanted to laugh as it all seemed so alien to my experience of Edinburgh and going on holiday in Corfu.

We were taken back into the airport and slowly, one by one, given our passports back and again we were relieved of some of our duty free. I am not sure if we had idiots marked across our foreheads, but it did look that night that many people were relieved of their duty free.

What a terrible pity because by golly we were going to be in need of it in the near future.

Well, a few hours later we all arrived in Nairobi. This was a lonely time. Catherine and Steve were staying in Kenya, I was flying on to Uganda. I left them both with tears in my eyes, tired and a bit fed up at being so tired. I rechecked my bags in and it was when I sat down I saw that I had been issued a boarding pass on a flight to Zambia. All I knew was that I was not going there; the lady reissued me a new ticket with no apparent fuss, but I had great fears for my suitcase, 20 kilos for 2 years, but all that 20 kilos was mine, with all my memories and photos, plus what I needed.

Well I did eventually arrive, as did my luggage, and was met by

Dad scoring a goal against East Fife

Clare and I at Christmas in Edinburgh

Edinburgh Royal Infirmary Sept 1975: my PTS nursing group

DIOCESE OF GULU	THIS IS TO CERTIFY THAT:

DIOCESE OF GULU
IDENTITY CARD

Name of Bearer (Block Letters)

MISS WAUDHAUGH JOANNE

Signature of Bearer: Joanne Waudhaugh

THIS IS TO CERTIFY THAT:

Rev./Mr./Mrs./Miss WAUDHAUGH JOANNE

is a Priest/Brother/Sister/Doctor NURSE
In a good standing in the Diocese, and is
Salaried/Unsalaried.

The above MISS WAUDHAUGH JOANNE

is employed by me in the Diocese, and is
presently domiciled at:

Address ST.MARY'S HOSPITAL LACOR
P.O.BOX 200 - GULU

Change of Address

Born 1957 Nationality BRITISH
Work Nurses Tutor

Certified under my seal:

† Cipriano Dr. Kihangire,
Bishop of Gulu

Gulu, Uganda: my ID card, required for travelling in Uganda

Left to right: Stan, Penny, Mary, Mark and Margaret on our
camping trip to Ruwenzori

Left to right: Angelina, Dorina, me kneeling, Joan and Margaret, at Gulu

Gulu: Drs Lucille & Pierro Corti, front row kneeling, and Sr Lina and myself standing far right, with doctors & visitors from Italy

Tanzania: heads out the bus for air on our journey from Kipalapala to Nairobi

The bus arriviving in Singida for a break

a smashing Irish Mill hill priest called Brendan Jordan, who would keep me sane and grounded in the coming times.

I was taken from Entebbe airport, letting my eyes pop out of my head when I saw the old Entebbe airport riddled with bullets. Of course this was the Entebbe/Israeli siege! Being there in front of that history seemed unreal to me. At that point Dora Bloggs' name came into my mind, as she was the only one of that group never to be seen again. We travelled along the Entebbe road and there were the beautiful mud huts. Everything seemed so unbelievable to me. It was fantastic, I was in Africa, it was powerful. The colour of the women walking on the road, their dresses were so pink and yellow and green and bright, they were beautiful. I saw soldiers with guns and there was a road block or two, but Brendan negotiated them painlessly. We were coming nearer Kampala city and there just seemed to be hundreds of people walking everywhere. Buildings in the town were riddled with bullets, but in my mind "that stuff was all over and done with" as Idi Amin had just been thrown out by the Tanzanians 3 months ago and President Beniisa was in charge.

I landed at the Italian Comboni convent where some nuns with broken English welcomed me warmly. They let me use their phone to let my mum know that I had arrived safely, which I did. It was an exciting time, here I was in Africa. I slept most of that day and got up in the evening to a lovely meal of rosemary rabbit. Little did I know that I would have the chance of eating rosemary rabbit every night for the next 2 years. The Combonis were magical when it came to self reliance and breeding their own rabbits was one way of surviving the war. Anyway, that first night I thought it was sumptuous.

I sat out on the balcony at about nine o'clock. Darkness falls every night at about 7 o'clock in Africa. There was a blast of gunfire. No one seemed to hear it. It rattled again, I looked at all the nuns continuing their conversation and embroidery. One of them looked at me and said, "Don't worry, its just gunfire, nowhere near us." I thought, well if they don't even hear it, I must have nothing to worry about.

That first night I slept well, I was full of delight that I had come to Africa, here I was, a missionary, hey hey, a bit like Gladys after all. There was no dilly dally, I was to get up to my mission as soon as possible and that morning after the car was packed full of provisions, Brendan came back and picked me up. This was exciting. We were to travel 3 to 4 hours north along one straight road to get to Gulu. I was to work in a hospital called St Mary's' Lacor. It was started by an Italian and French Canadian couple called the Cortis, both doctors and both seasoned livers in Africa. There would be no nonsense taken from them seemingly. You were there for a job, not a holiday, and if you did not work then why stay. That was OK with me as I intended to work.

The road from Kampala to Gulu was amazing, it was just red and dusty. The trees were wonderful flat topped trees you see in pictures of Africa and we saw the occasional monkey along the road. We went straight there and after a few hours we safely landed in Gulu. It was here I handed over what was left of my duty free to Brendan. He took the whiskey and the cigarettes. I kept my own cheroots to keep me sane. The whiskey and cigs appeared at every VMM party we had. Brendan was great, when our supply fell, which it did very rapidly, he helped us through with wine and various spirits he could get his hands on for us. He was a bit of a great priest come artful dodger!

There were 2 women VMMs, Margaret and Joan at a nearby school and 2 guy VMMs, Stan and Mark at a nearby seminary teaching English and the likes. It was great, we came together every week where possible to gather, have mass together with Brendan and eat and drink. It was always fantastic to see how creative we could all be with very little. Ice cream made from tins of Nestles milk, chocolate made from potatoes mashed with icing sugar and essence of coffee, it was mad, but I still had to face the first few days on the mission compound in Lacor.

The matron met me, her name was Sr Lina, she was a tired looking kind woman who had big working hands. She told me they had nowhere for me to stay yet but I had a lovely room with a shower and toilet of my own in the nurses' home. That was fine, I was a missionary and be happy with your lot. The room was grand and I was excited to see around the hospital.

I was taken aside and told that the nurse tutor was going to be leaving any day now and would I mind taking over her position running the nursing school of about 70 state enrolled student nurses; and their London board exams would be in 6 months time, which would give me enough time to settle into the job. I must have looked so vacant that she continued to explain. The tutor was of the West Nile tribe, which was Idi Amin's tribe. The nurses who were not of that tribe hated the tutor, as she was a bully when Amin was in power. The previous week the nurses had allegedly organised the soldiers to make an ambush to kill her. This attempt was foyled, but now she was to leave the compound secretly one night to save herself. The vacant look must have disappeared, but been replaced by the fish look. All I could do was open my mouth and close it and then I felt a terrible urge to laugh. It was all so alien, I had visions of some of our tutors in Edinburgh whom we did not like, the worst we ever did was fall asleep in their class, but to try and assassinate your tutor because they were of a wrong tribe! Well, what was even funnier was that I was to replace her!

I was told that she was a very angry person just now who did not want to help anyone who was taking over from her. I said that I was not a qualified tutor or anything, I just loved teaching practical skills. I was told not to mention that, but that you did need access to all their student numbers for the exams and any other information needed to continue working in the school. That afternoon I was introduced to a very angry serious looking lady who had no intention of helping me one little bit. Part of me felt like putting on the little girl from Edinburgh routine, but I reckoned this lady would demolish me. I had to grow up and open my eyes to the seriousness of the situation around me and to the fact that you believe that you are going to be loved and welcomed just because you decided to do something helpful with yourself. I rapidly realised that this was not going to be the case. If you were around then so what and if you were not around then so what. I sat outside her office for the next three whole days waiting for her to make up her mind to see me. I had been told to expect a different pace of life in Africa so this must be it.

I kept trying to tell myself that I was not being lazy and this was all part of being a missionary. Sr Lina seemed to approve of my patience as seemingly did the Cortis so I must be doing something correct. I felt bad though, because everyone else seemed to be so very, very busy in the hospital. On the 4th day, the tutor called me into her office and interviewed me and asked me to write down my qualifications on a piece of paper. I mustered up every course I had done and all my qualifications with numerous letters after each. It was all received with silence. I was then given a timetable and told I would start the anatomy, pharmacy and practical classes tomorrow. I nearly died! She was taking all her books and there was no library in this war torn part of the globe. I smiled graciously and thanked her for her help. The door was locked and that was me. I belted around all the Italian nuns for books and then went to the local school for biology books. I actually had brought one of my own nursing books with me so, that night was a long night in preparing my classes. I arrived at the school the next day. There was no Tutor, she was gone and I prayed safely this time, all the keys were in the locks of the drawers. This was my first office and in about 10 minutes would be my first class.

I walked into the class where I saw a sea of faces looking at me. They were so bright, sharp and smiling. I opened my class book, introduced myself and started. The class was supposed to last one hour and to my horror there was nothing left to say after 20 minutes. I had finished.

I looked at their blank faces, I asked if anyone understood what I said, there was not a stir of expression, they had not understood one word. I was nervous so I had spoken very fast in my broad Edinburgh accent. NOT ONE WORD did they understand and Oh God I couldn't go through that class again. I stopped, I slowed way down and started to open up real communication, I saw in their expression now that I was changing enough to let them get my accent. I did not do too much that day bar try and open up lines of true communication. Me trying to understand their accents and them trying to understand me. Oh what fun. Thankfully because I was living in the nurses' home and had no cooking facilities, I ate with the doctors who were mainly Italian. Their food was supplied by the convent. It was rosemary rabbit and salami!

I spent every evening working hard on keeping one class ahead of all the three classes I gave. The VMM teachers gave me a hand in making lesson plans and teaching. Any tips were very welcome. The practical classes were hilarious. I had been given a wonderful staff nurse to help me with basically everything from culture of the Ugandan people to helping with the administration. This girl was amazing and a true God send. I asked her to set up some of the practical classes for the morning as I was up to my eye balls with corrections. In Edinburgh we had everything packed for us and I had no idea which end of an instrument was what, I prayed that Angelina did. I walked into my first practical class with all the instruments set up by Angelina. I went round the class asking each one in turn what the name of the instruments were, whilst trying to remember them all myself for future classes. The girls were very serious and very worried that I was being very strict with them, little did they know that I knew very little about some tropical procedures that needed to be done. I was like a sponge. Learning, learning, learning all the time and most important, retaining everything. The girls were wonderful and I was building up a good rapport with them. One great compliment I was given was by a 2nd year student who thought I was the bees knees. She said," Ah Miss Joanne, you are very white and very fat!" She was thrilled with giving me such a compliment, I on the contrary decided to try and get a tan and lose some weight.

After a very short time I knew that to learn and retain you need to learn whilst practicing. I decided to take part of the curriculum up to the wards. Hopefully if the girls learnt well on the ward they would transmit that learning to the pages of their examinations papers. On to the wards I went. Lacor was a large enough hospital with satellite hospitals all over the north of Uganda. At a push it would hold 200 to 300 patients at a time. There were surgical, medical, gynae and children's wards and units. To my new naive eyes it was all quite shocking. The smell of infected wounds was everywhere, even though there was a very good level of cleaning going on. There was no disposable anything. Nothing is disposable in Africa. Absolutely everything can be reused some how. Needles, syringes, intravenous bottles, bandages gathered from wounds, washed and sterilized. Nothing was wasted, paper bags, small plastic bottles, all used for dispensing medicines in war time. Some of the needles had a certain amount of bluntness to them, but at times that was all we had. Medicines were limited so used wisely, many diseases were rampant and devastating. Malaria was a sure killer when children got it. Their haemoglobin levels would fall to such a low level that they went into cardiac arrest. Measles wiped out hundreds, their little bodies being unable to retain fluids due to the sores from the measles all down their enteric tract. Severe malnutrition was everywhere. Marasmus and kwashiorkor were the two main malnutrition killers. One was a severe lack of protein in the diet, the other just a severe lack of food. Both conditions were nearly impossible to cure. The reason for such malnutrition at that time was civil unrest and war. Food was planted and violence erupted. To save your lives you had to flee to the bush. It was either too unsafe to go back home, so you had to forage food from the forest, or you went home and the soldiers had helped themselves to the harvest. People were on the run and, to add to it, if there was drought the crop was not good and there was no back up from the last harvest. People struggled to survive in some areas, it was pitiful to see.

Another common disease was syphilis and gonorrhoea. Soldiers were forever stopping us at gunpoint demanding Tetracycline which could help treat STDs. I realised that any time in any country that there is civil unrest or war, all the sexually transmitted infection rate will rise. Uganda was no exception. Tropical ulcers were very common. They were dreadfully slow to heal and extremely painful. I was amazed how quickly they can appear and spread. Dust and flies were great spreaders. TB was rampant, bilharzias common and serious worm infestation regular. I was amazed at the children's ward as there were often 3 to a bed. Food was supplemented by the hospital, but the relatives had to look after as much as they could. The children were fed and the relatives looked after all the toiletries care of the patient. It took a while to get my head round all of that, but I had to get used to it.

Food was so difficult to get. I myself was having withdrawals and was really getting sick of eating rosemary rabbit. Luckily every week we, the VMMs, got together for a "party" of sorts and tried frying some of the root vegetables. We had chipped matoke, chipped cassava and chipped sweet potatoes. Getting a chicken to eat was a real treat and I remember the girls telling us we had a chicken for our Friday get together. It was hilarious. I was blessed that I had no false teeth as if you did you would have lost them on that chicken. Margaret and Joan had boiled it for hours to take the "bounce" out of it, then roasted it for a few hours, too. The result was a chicken you could have proudly played tennis with. We all, though, valiantly pulled and stretched at the chicken till it was "all gone". Happily we washed it all down with a glass of whiskey supplied by Brendan.

Most nights were uneventful and you wouldn't go out as it was too dangerous after dark. Most nights I contented myself with the rabbit and was thankful for it and spent the evening chatting to the Italian doctors. They were a mad bunch and I enjoyed their company. Of course they all spoke Italian and so at times I felt desperately home sick to have a good "blether". I ate and drank with the Italians at the top of the compound, but to get back to the nurses home I had to cross a field where there were three vicious alsatians trained to bite. I tried most nights to get back before they were let out, but one night I stayed longer than normal. I was crossing the fields when I heard the barking and growling of the dogs. The night watchman would usually see it was me and call the dogs off. This night, however, the dogs were not called off and they kept running. I could see all three of them coming like bullets towards me, teeth bared. I shouted at the top of my voice for the night watchman Pasqually, but he was nowhere to be seen. The dogs landed on me and it was horrific. One put his teeth into my right calf and was growling, the other put one paw on my right shoulder and one paw on my left shoulder. His face barked and growled into mine. The other ran round and round in circles barking like a rabid dog. I could not breath, I could not cry, I could not scream, I could not move. The night watchman was not around and I thought I could not hold my nerve for much longer, I just wanted to collapse with fear. Eventually, Pasqually came wandering over the field and called the three of them off me. I was unable to speak, but staggered into the nurses' home where I collapsed in the toilet. All I could think of was that coming back late to the nurses' home in Edinburgh was not so traumatic; at worst you would get a ticking off, here I felt I almost lost my life!

After that the Italians took it in turn to walk me home and as one of them said "stone the dogs." It was found that if they were running at you and you threw a few rocks in the right direction they would flee. However, I took an Italian doctor home every night, I always thought that sounded good!

I had been in Uganda now for three months and I loved it. I had listened to stories about the withdrawal of Idi Amin's troops along the Gulu road that were truly frightening and horrific. I had been moved over to the Italian side of the compound to a tiny bed sit of my own. I had the possibility of getting a kitchen of my own at some point. Dry bread, thick coffee and salami for breakfast was also getting me down. I would do anything for a bowl of cornflakes or real toast with real butter and marmalade. My bed sit was grand, it had a small sitting room with a door to the bedroom and toilet. Above me was Dr Dorina who had just arrived and next to her was Enrico and Marcelina. I loved those two, one was a doctor and one a nurse. I could go any time and chat with them, they spoke English with me as I slowly learnt to hear the Italian conversations.

It was with Enrico and Marcelina that I experienced my first fried flying ant. Flying ants came out at certain season and they were a fantastic source of protein. Many people just popped them in raw and crunched, I never had the nerve to do that. Marceline made some fried and she said just pop them in. I did, they were crunchy and fishy tasting. I was proud of myself. Later on I found another way to eat such a rich source of protein was to pound them and if you used your imagination it almost tasted like peanut butter.

Around this time I started to run out of a lot of things, the basic such as nice smelly soap, deodorants, toothpaste, loo rolls, booze and my cheroots. It is hard to imagine that there were no shops up our way. Oil, matches and soap were sold, but precious little else.

Once a week I was allowed to borrow the Comboni Brothers' motor bike or piki piki, to go into Gulu town to get some shopping. I did not need much but had decided to cook for myself at the weekends and had waited to get in a gas cylinder. I loved having fried egg and matoke chips, it was great. I also decided not to tell my Nana that I was riding around Uganda on a motor bike. I got caught a good few times with buying rotten eggs. There is nothing more disastrous than that, God the smell really is awful, but it did not put me off my Saturday fry up. Eventually I would take in my own saucepan and fill it with water and check that the eggs did not float. So after a while the amount of rotten eggs I bought decreased.

Life went on and just over a month into my time in Uganda there was a bloodless coup in Kampala. President Beniisa was overthrown and the military took over.Paulo Muwanga, Obotes right hand man was appointed chair of the military commission which governed Uganda for the next 6 months leading up to the elections. Within a short time Obote came back from Tanzania... Life was on the verge of change from this point onwards.

UGANDAN COUP

I was quite proud of myself. Imagine I could brag that I had been through a military coup, it sounded impressive, even though it was a bloodless one at that. I knew folk at home would be worried and I wrote my weekly letter home saying all was well. Letters from home came through about every 6 weeks and it was the biggest boost of the week when you received them. There was no phone link from Gulu so I really did rely on post. My mum was brilliant. She had a method of every day popping a line or two down in her notepad of what went on during the week, then at the end of the week I got a full report. Mum did this for all the time I spent in Africa.

Well, life went on as usual and I was beginning to enjoy teaching the nurses and now of course I had my own wee pad and did not have to face the ordeal of "stoning the dogs" every night. The only other trial was mosquitoes. Not only do they spread malaria, but have a wonderful knack of keeping you awake at night. You may be dosing off then the next thing you were woken up abruptly with a spitfire attack into your ear. You ended up lashing out at the dark, putting a pillow over your head and trying to fall asleep again only to find out this time you are too hot to sleep, remove the pillow only to be dive bombed again and again. The night was truly disturbed when you had to put the light on, find an old newspaper, grit your teeth in fury and swipe about like someone trying to send SOS signals to the other end of the world. Eventually, exhausted and often defeated by the valiant mossy, you gave up, only to wake up the next morning covered in bites and waiting to see if you would get malaria.

One night, I went to bed as usual and fell into a deep fitful sleep only to be woken up by the most awful rain falling on the tin roof, it was so unbelievably loud that it woke me right up from a deep sleep. I sat up and thought I don't have a tin roof above me, Dr Dorina is above me. What on earth could that deafening noise be, it sounded like what I could only imagine was heavy gunfire. My heart pounded out my chest as at that very minute I knew it was gunfire because the banshee screams that accompanied the bullets confirmed my fears. I lost my breath for a second and my legs would not move for another. I got up and went to the only door I had to look out. It was very early dawn. I stuck my nose out the door only to have to shut it as quick. The gunfire seemed to be pointing in my direction and there were hundreds of soldiers breaking into the compound and shooting what looked like everything in sight. It is amazing what you actually see in a glance because many of the soldiers seemed to be running back to the road with women over their shoulders. I picked up my long handled brush and hid in my long green nightdress behind the door. This seemed a ridiculous place to stand just waiting on them to come and get me. I ran into the bedroom and looked out the only side window I had. I could hear THUMP THUMP THUMP down the side of the window and knew that they were going to come and "get me". Suddenly my mind went blank, I did not want to think what "get me" meant. At that point I realised that they were not footsteps outside but my own heart was beating so loudly I heard it outside of myself.

I knew in an instant two things. One, I did not want to die alone and two, I did not want to be found in my nightdress by the soldiers. I quickly threw a dress on top of my nighty, flung on flip flops and decided to make a run upstairs to Dorina's place then cut through to Enrico and Marcilina's. Would I make it up the stairs without getting shot? I did not know, but I really knew that to die alone like that would be horrendous. Headlines from the Edinburgh evening news flashed through my mind saying, "Edinburgh nurse killed in Ugandan massacre." I felt sorry for my mum seeing that. Anyway I had to chance it, and get upstairs. I suddenly felt like John Wayne running around a cowboy movie dodging the bullets. I had Dorina's spare house key in my hand and then one, two, three, I ran like the wind out and up the stairs three or four at a time. Bullets were whizzing by but thankfully none "got me".

I flew into Dorina's house and she screamed, flung the lights on then nearly died with relief at seeing me. I switched the light off fast and after a quick hug of friendship said, "Lets go through to be with Enrico." She had the adjoining key to their apartment and we flew in there, only to be greeted by this huge Italian man wielding an enormous axe. We screamed at him that it was only us and with one hand, he grabbed me and Dorina, shoved us into his bedroom where Marcelina was sitting cross legged. Enrico shut the door, held the axe in the ready position and laughed saying this is one way to attract so many women. Only a marvellous guy like Enrico could say such a thing at such a time.

We sat there the three of us on the bed listening to the awful screaming. The African sisters' convent was being attacked and we impotently listened to their screaming. Time moved on, the sun rose, the screaming and bullets stopped making noise. We sat and held out breath. The door opened and in walked Sr Lina, the big wholesome Comboni nun, telling us the soldiers had left now in their lorries and the compound was secure. We were all still left in the dark as to what had happened. The African sisters had "just" been terrorised, one staff nurse had been shot and many of their belongings taken, but no one killed. The villagers outside the compound came streaming into the hospital all day beaten and broken. They told us that when Idi Amin's troops fled out of Uganda through Gulu town, some of the Lacor villagers had looted parts of Gulu and the military base. The new soldiers were just retaliating and letting all of us know now who was boss.

I couldn't believe that, I was so frightened and all I wanted to do was go home, but when seeing the state of everyone else who had been through so much the previous year, I felt a wimp. I went to the classroom that morning all ready with my lessons for the day. My mind was blank though and I could not concentrate or stand still. I actually felt rather hyper. Luckily, the wise matron, Sr Lina, plodded into the classroom and told me to cancel classes, the groundnuts needed harvesting. None of us needed to be asked twice and we spent the rest of the day in the fields picking the nuts. That was a brilliant day, we spent it together and we got a lot of our fears out on the land. Fresh ground nuts are amazing, they are so different from hard nuts which have dried. Fresh nuts are as good as sweet meat. I was learning all the time.

That night Enrico and Marcelina asked me to stay upstairs with them as they knew I must be feeling frightened. I shrugged it off and said I have to stand on my own two feet again some time. I sat up in my bed all night long listening for the sound of "heavy rain" to come, I did that for three nights in a row until exhaustion caught up with me and I realised that this was life in Uganda.

There was a general air of disquiet in the compound. Tribalism kept poking its head up, girls stayed with their tribes, totally distrusting each other. This was a serious thing to occur especially if they were meant to nurse the patients as a team. Most nights now there was gunfire either from the military barracks or from further looting in the villages. I learnt to sleep through these noises as they were a mile or two away from us, we would only see the consequences in the morning.

After the military coup, road blocks were set up all over the place. Between Gulu and Kampala there were nine. Your journey depended on how much the soldiers had been drinking as to whether they would give you a hard time or not. The hard times were very unpleasant and unpredictable, the good times when they were not drinking were nerve wracking. After a while you got blasé about how to treat them, always smile and let them know they are the boss and they are very good people. Some of the soldiers were good people, only they were starving and received no pay. Amin's soldiers were trained military, these lads were just lads with no training and they had serious weapons on them which was frightening.

There was generalized tension all over the country and when Amin threatened to come back to Uganda through Zaire, we knew we were in trouble. Gulu was in the North and would be on route to the main highway up to Zaire. That meant all the troops from Gulu barracks were being sent up the Zaire road to block Amin's attempted return.

Another VMM called Mary came to the compound to help in the school and the hospital, it was great to have the company and we were given a new house together on the other side of the compound, away from both the nurses' home and the Italians. It meant too, that we were on our own for cooking now as this place had a kitchen, it was going to be fun trying to cook with nothing. Mary was a character, salt of the earth person, she loved the cigarettes and enjoyed a drink when possible, she looked like a good omen for me and we forged a binding friendship thankfully.

One night at around 2pm in the morning, the whole compound was woken up and told to get up to the hospital, all hands on deck, so get there quick. As we arrived there, lorries came pouring into the mission compound. I stayed with the lorries and became triage nurse. The first few bodies were definitely dead and we put them to one side. Then I was handed a leg, then a boot with a foot in it, how strange I thought. There were a few men alive and seriously wounded and I moved them up for theatre as quickly as possible. There were more dead men and bits of bodies falling out of the lorries and there were a few, badly shocked with small injuries, who just needed help, sent to the dressing clinics set up on the ward, until they too would eventually see a doctor.

One of these walking wounded handed me a little cloth bag. I opened it and it was full of fingers, loads of them, they all fell down my front as I breath takingly let the whole bag fall. I gave a shudder and knew I wasn't going to pick them all up so I got on with the job in hand, making sure the illest amongst these soldiers would get seen first.

The night went fast. Everyone had a job. I had to go round and make sure all who came in got their tetanus injections. Tetanus was a terrible disease which still occurs with frequency, so that second job took me a while. There were others, putting drips up, giving antibiotics, temporary dressings and the theatre going hell for leather. The doctors were fantastic and so expert. We all worked round the clock. Classes of course were cancelled and by late afternoon the next day things seemed to be more under control.

These men had been up north to fight the advancing Amin troops. They had been ambushed, blown up and shot at. They had been sitting ducks really. At that moment, on the ward, a very high ranking military officer barged in. Just his general presence was intimidating with his pistol showing proudly by his side. He told me to find a bible. There were always plenty on a mission compound and I gave him one. He made every man in that ward and the next ward put their hands up towards the bible and he swore them all into the Ugandan army and walked out. One man said to me, "how can he do that, I am a Muslim." I thought, "How can he do that, just send boys up to face Amin's troops, not sworn into the army, no training or military experience and not even sure how to shoot a gun, then when they are all blown to shreds swear them into the Ugandan army." I was GOB SMACKED.

Over the next few weeks more lads came trickling in after being attacked, but not in such high quantities. We were all able to cope with our normal duties and help out with the casualties.

THE REALITY OF WAR

It was now that I began to learn what war was all about. I had now had my first encounter with dumb dumb bullets, which I was told were banned by the Geneva convention. Most of our boys had been decimated by the dumb dumbs. They explode on contact with the person or object. Many of their legs needed amputation because they were splintered to bits by these outrageous bullets, and I was learning that this is a fact of war. Do as much damage in any way possible and don't mind the rules. I also learnt that politics and gun running are number one in the world. People and regimes are disposable if there is money involved. In situations like this there are powers working that are higher than we can ever imagine or be able to change. All we could do was deal with the reality in front of us and not think too much.

One night a soldier came in badly hurt with head injuries. His brain was swelling and bleeding. They needed to do Burr holes in the scalp to relieve the pressure. The senior doctors (The Cortis) were away for the day at another hospital. The new Italian doctors had never done Burr holes but understood it needed to be done. I was to sit at the top of the theatre and read out the procedure step by step whilst they did the op'. It was successful and I do know that that man survived. I often felt as though we were a unit from Mash. I wondered to Mary which one of us was going to be "Hot Lips Houlahan!"

There was an 8pm curfew established and on the whole most people kept to it. We still attempted to have our weekly get together as VMM, but it was becoming increasingly dangerous to travel. Skirmishes were common, shooting and bombing at night were common, too. Most times we slept well as we were too tired to do otherwise. You might be woken up by shooting and screaming, but if it wasn't in the compound you fell asleep again. Uganda was dangerous, but we all had jobs to get on with. It was a strange privilege to be part of this country's journey.

I laughed with the poor Italians who at that time had two choices in life. One was military service for two years and the other was

My bedsit accommodation, Gulu, bottom right, with the steps
leading to Dorina's flat and next door to Enrico and Marcillina's

A party in our house with Enrico and Mary

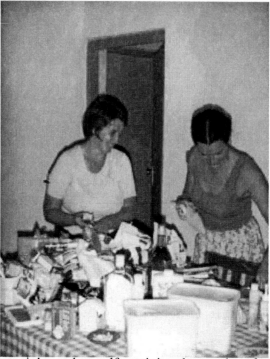

Gulu: Mary, right, and myself receiving the tea chest from home full of goodies

Ethiopia: the road to Chencha

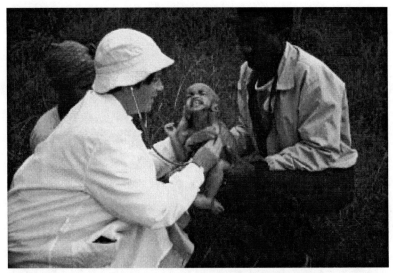

Ethiopia: checking a malnourished child for pneumonia at a clinic
in Chencha Hills

A malnourished child at the clinic. The little tuft of hair is for the
angels to collect the soul of the child with ease when dead

Ethiopia: on Lake Chamo where Mum and I "balanced the boat"

Ethiopia: Sr Paula, centre, and myself, far left, with the mission team outside our medical stores in Chencha

Third World experience for two years. The doctors had chosen a Third World experience so as not to experience war and now they realised that most of them were seeing more action than if they had chosen the military option. It was such irony. We all realised that there is no such thing as a clean war. War is dirty and the gloves come off very rapidly. Subtly, that changes your perspective in life.

We knew that there were going to elections held in Uganda in December. The main candidate was Milton Obote. He was from the Langi tribe and was a protestant man. I did not know too much more about him, but tribalism and religious division seemed to raise its ugly head. Obote was head of the UPC party which was protestant and Paul Kawanga Ssemogerere was head of the DP party and was Catholic. I had never experienced religious division in Edinburgh and found it frightening here in Uganda at this moment in time to be under threat because we were a catholic mission living with the Acholi tribe The girls were feeling the threat, too; more so due to tribalism. My aim was to try and keep unity between us all and not let these political and religious demons destroy us.

Brendan and another priest called Evert asked us all to meet. We had our VMM meeting that weekend in our house. We were told by Evert that there could be bloodshed coming and some of that blood could be ours and were we willing to stay? It was a very solemn decision to make at 23, but my decision, as was Mary's, was to stay. I reflected on my friends and life in Edinburgh. At that moment the contrast of my two lives were poles apart. At this moment in Uganda there were only two things - life or death, and all things figured around these two things.

Joan, Margaret, Stan, Mark and Brendan were all due their holidays, so they left for a few months, leaving Mary, Evert and myself. Life was lonely. We missed going out to the parties and the Comboni Missionaries asked us if we would confine ourselves to barracks for the next few months as it was just far too dangerous. They were right, too. Seemingly there was a hit list going around. There was a sister Joanne's name on it as she was quite vocal. Someone came up to me and asked me was I not worried that they would shoot me because we had the same name! I hadn't thought of that up till then. Indeed, the Combonis were right, stay in and we might get through this.

Rations were low at this time. We went across the road on a Saturday to the local market. Going into town was too dangerous now. We were incredibly inventive with our root vegetables and tomatoes. We ran out of salt too, but were taught to make a replacement with ash. I became a smoker then, too. My cheroots had long ago run out, as had Mary's cigarettes. We found real tobacco leaves in the village and would buy a bundle. Mary was great at this, but she would take two leaves and dry them bone dry in the sun, de-vein them, then sit crushing the dry tobacco till it was really powdery. She would then add a very small touch of the local booze called "waragi", blend that in and that would be her supply for a few days. We ran out of Rizzla paper regularly so descended onto our precious letters to roll the tobacco in. It is amazing how well it did the job and amazing how blue our lips became when the ink came off.

These three months before the December elections were really tough. We felt claustrophobic, isolated, young and in need of some fun, we were desperate to get out. However, self preservation won the day and we continued rolling our own cigarettes and drinking the local booze laced with lemons!

December 1980 arrived. The elections were being held and everyone was literally holding their breath. The tension was palpable. One morning I was in class when an armed soldier burst in and pointed his gun at me. Some guns went off in the compound, but I realised that the soldiers had just dropped their rifles by mistake, no one was hit that time. The soldier told me he was removing the nurses from the classroom. Sr Lina came in behind him and quickly told me to let them go, he was taking them at gun point to vote and if they all voted for Milton Obote then they would all come back safely. I couldn't believe this. I had heard on the BBC that morning that there were free and fair elections being held in Uganda! Well if this is free and fair then I would not like to guess what was corrupt. After an hour or so the girls all came walking back with armed escort. They were solemn and silent. I thought the best course of action was tea and lots of it. I knew now that if Obote was not

38

elected, we were dead. We were white, catholic and certainly of the wrong tribe. Our mission had treated Amin's soldiers and for that we would be seriously penalized. We just hoped he would get in for our sakes.

A couple of days went by and all the country had voted. We were all expecting the results within two to three days. We waited, barely able to concentrate, but determined to smoke our guts out. Indeed, Mary had been given a recent present of real cigarettes, soon we would hopefully have something to celebrate and smoke them, too.

On December the 8th 1980, just 9 months after leaving home in Edinburgh, we were told to go to our houses and may God be with us all. We had been told to leave the doors closed but unlocked, as it was more terrifying hearing soldiers breaking in, just let them in without the frenzy and they may just steal everything and not touch you. We thought that sound advice!

The silence was sickeningly eerie. Not even the cocks were crowing, it was as though not only were the humans holding their breath but so were the animals. The silence was frightening. Every hour on the hour we turned on the radio to listen to the BBC. They kept repeating that all was well in Kampala and there appeared to be free and fair elections.

The noise erupted suddenly. It sounded like villagers chanting themselves into a frenzy, the noise was worse than the silence. The awful screaming and shouting and chanting was making its way to the Mission compound. We had armed soldiers surrounding the compound but, after a short burst of gunfire, we heard the level of frenzied screaming increase and thumping and bashing the main steal doors of the compound. We were told, I cannot remember by whom, that the villagers were coming to wipe us out with their spears and pangas. Why? Because we were white Catholic and had treated Amin's soldiers. I really started to pray that I would get shot in the head that day, I did not want to die by machete. We turned the 4 o'clock BBC news on to hear our fate as all seemed to be so confused. The headlines read, "John Lennon was shot dead in New York."

I was furious beyond words. Who gave a damn about John Lennon when we were on the verge of being massacred. I was full of rage as there was now no news about Uganda on the radio. We were totally cut off and I felt no one cared about Uganda's plight. This terrible attack on the compound lasted till near 6pm when all of a sudden all hell broke loose. The villagers scattered, there were no more drums and chanting and spear throwing. The bazookas took over with very heavy gun fire from all directions. It was a dreadful noise but I felt quite relieved that now I would die by the gun.

Mary and I decided to go and see what was happening and see if they needed help in the hospital. Bombings, bazookas and soldiers were everywhere and as we arrived in the hospital I saw one doctor getting clobbered round the ear by a soldier. Ill soldiers who were on bed rest or were wired up to contraptions on the bed due to broken bones were trying to escape. There was bedlam on the wards. Nobody knew anything, the bed ridden soldiers thought they were going to be murdered in their beds and were trying to escape, we thought we were all for the chop and we hoped that these bazookas would not land on us. Madness was all around us.

Mary and I met with Sr Lina who said there was nothing for us to do but try and keep safe, no one knew what was happening and there was no news anywhere about Uganda due to John Lennon's death. Mary and I said we would stay with the nurses in the nurses' home that night, because if the soldiers got into the compound they would be targets. Maybe if we were there we could talk sense to them. Sounds ridiculous now, but we wanted to be with them.

We needed rations for the night. We went back to our "open" house and collected the box of Mary's "good" cigarettes. It was the longest night ever. We sat cross legged, fully clothed on a bed near the door. We chain smoked the whole night. The gunfire stopped early morning, but the soldiers were all around the compound and we could hear them. We hoped everyone was safe. Some of the nurses had wanted to hide in the bush and take their chances there, they felt safer out than in.

Mary was great, I was much more frightened than her, but I do remember her saying that she thought she should feel more scared.

Anyway by 6am all was quiet. Nurses came out of their rooms. We all had survived, we all hoped all was well in the other parts of the compound. The Church was the meeting ground for us all. It was great seeing everyone safe and sound there as we all trickled in for mass.

It was in the morning that we heard that Milton Obote was now President of Uganda and all last night the soldiers were just celebrating their victory. Luckily for us, as the villagers had been on a rampage and were setting out to do some blood letting.

Classes went on as usual that morning. We were all tired I suppose, but Mary and I were hyped up on nicotine and caffeine so we were fit to tackle the next 24hours head on. There were a lot of general injuries. People had been beaten up, women raped and some taken away to the barracks. I believe these poor souls were let out after two days of sexual gratification by the soldiers. Some soldiers came in shell shocked and it was later on in the day we saw Mary in action. I was leaving the hospital and speaking to some of the doctors about their day when we heard roaring and shouting. We could all see into the hospital ward were Mary was tackling a shell shocked patient. One minute he was sitting up, the next minute Mary seemed to hold him down for his own safety. It was an up/down scenario and looked just like a Monty Python sketch. I felt like shouting, "Way to go Mary," but we all ended up laughing hysterically instead.

A couple of weeks after the elections Evert and I were needing to go to Kampala for supplies, and also a break out of the compound. We were two hours into the journey when we were stopped at an unofficial road block. There were 6 lorries on the road ahead of us. We waited and watched in silence as the soldiers emptied the bodies from the trucks and dumped them all into a swamp. We watched. When they had finished the job they moved us on. We never looked left or right but straight ahead.

Coming back from Kampala, Evert had obviously marked the spot. We stopped and prayed and I presume Evert blessed the bodies. We never really talked about it, maybe my mind would have blown if I had. We moved on.

Life was full of busyness and most nights there was local shooting

41

and looting. Obote's soldiers were bullies and very undisciplined. They were frightening as all they did around our area was drink and intimidate. Many people were just killed during that time. At one stage 10 soldiers came into the hospital very ill. 5 died on admission and the other 5 were critically ill and were blind. It seemed a puzzle to me but was very clear to them, they had been poisoned by the local brew called "waragi". Two more of the soldiers died and their friends went on the hunt for the person who sold them the drink.

The story went as follows. One old widow had recently lost her son to the soldiers killing him. She wanted revenge and knew the soldiers bought her waragi. She deliberately did not distil it which was a lethal thing to do. She deliberately wanted to kill as many soldiers as she could. The soldiers found her, took her back to the barracks and forced her to drink her own brew, when she was near to death they shot her and dumped her body.

The soldiers were out of control and could in their daily drunken rage kill as many people as they wanted. One day a group of soldiers crashed their jeep into a group of villagers doing their shopping, many were killed, the soldiers were not disciplined. One day another group of soldiers crashed into a lorry. People were squashed beneath the load. It was the only thing in Africa that nearly made me faint. The bodies underneath were completely flattened, there were no contours, they looked like paper cut outs. The soldiers were not disciplined.

The Bishop of Gulu made a complaint against the soldiers. I was delighted that someone had done something, but terrified when I heard that President Obote wanted to see every head of department in the hospital. I couldn't believe that I was to go, but I had to. There was about 8 of us and there was a great silence as we entered the room and sat down. I was sitting opposite the Bishop, which I thought was quite a dangerous place to be. I also kept thinking, how strange, I haven't been in this country for a full year yet and here I am a 23 year old Edinburgh girl, who just wanted to do something with her life for a year or two, being brought into a very sinister meeting with the President of Uganda.

Obote came into the room and sat at the head of the room. He was a very dark man and had eyes that were hard to look at. I didn't want to look at them and I had an awful sense of evil in his presence. He overtly threatened us all saying if we complained again we could all disappear like Father Martin has(I have changed his name to respect his annonaminity). We all knew that a local priest had disappeared and we presumed taken by the soldiers. I thought "That's fine, I won't open my mouth again, let me go." However, just as I was thinking that to myself the Bishop spoke up and started to argue with Obote about his unruly soldiers. I was proud yet terrified of what the Bishop was doing. Obote just ended it and warned us all.

I needed a drink! The crowd had come back from holiday and had brought booze, cigarettes and even a few cheroots. Curfew was still in place but I would walk through the forest at the back of the mission to get there. Mary and I had a mission and that was to party. It was strange hearing all the news from home and there was a new VMM who had replaced Joan. I now felt like one of the gang. I'd been through the elections and survived.

When new people came they really seemed strange. They all had nice haircuts for one thing and usually smelt nice. They had their supply of shampoo and deodorants which gave a welcomed change to the usual lux soap we all had. Soon the nice smells would disappear and the sharp haircut would be replaced by a trim from someone every now and then. There was an innocence regarding evil in the world. I think that was the difference. After one year I felt a completely different person.

LIFE, AND HOLIDAYS, IN UGANDA

We all settled into the Uganda that was, daily shootings and stories of nasty road blocks, but it all seemed sort of hum drum stuff, that's just what life was and there was no big deal. One Comboni sister had just come back from her holidays and she was shot dead in her car travelling to her mission. One of the doctors was shot in his car, too, when he was out on safari doing some medical work. Going on the roads was getting dangerous, front seat passengers were most at risk. A bullet to the driver's head and the car was yours.

Mary and I needed to celebrate something. We did. Stan and Mark had somehow miraculously organised a tea chest of stuff for us, to be sent with one of the missionaries' medicines consignment. They had phoned my family and asked did they want to send us out some stuff. Well, they all came up trumps, new clothes, nice soaps, Mrs Black's shortbread (she was a good friend of the family and had made homemade short bread for me) and five home brew kits. God bless them all! Mary got a pile of stuff, too, and we opened the shortbread; well, we were all cheering Mrs Black, "God bless her!" Her shortbread was fantastic.

Mary and I had some serious business ahead of us and that was how to make the home brew! Stan and Mark knew there was an old empty deserted brewery in Gulu town, they were going to go in and get some bottles. They did and arrived with two crates of empties. Yes, we were on the road. I knew I could get a baby bath from the school of nursing demonstration class and an unused rectal tube needed to stop an explosion. We meticulously blended the brew, put it in the baby bath, covered it all over and stuck in the rectal tube to disperse the fumes. All we had to do was wait. We washed and sterilized the bottles and four weeks or so later we were ready. We needed sugar and Stan and Mark supplied that, too. We were ready to bottle. We got a great routine going. Mary would put in a teaspoon of sugar into each bottle while I filled them up; Mary then was bottler. We had a supply of caps and a capper, Mary just hammered down the cap to the bottle. We lost only one bottle and were very proud of our manufacture line.

We had to wait another few weeks then we had a party. All the nuns from the mission along the road came, all the Italian doctors, too. In war torn Uganda we were having a party. Most of us had not tasted beer for a while, so it was strong and went to our heads. The first toast was "God bless the family and Mrs Black" even though we had long finished the shortbread! We had four more packs which meant four more parties. We decided though to give the doctors a brew for themselves. Bottles were hard to get so they suggested the glass intravenous bottles would do. Indeed, we were becoming more like MASH every day!

Mary and I had split the teaching sessions up for the day. She was taking on the afternoon sessions and this gave me the afternoon off. I was delighted, I was free and I had transport! My plans were to go five miles up the road to the local junior seminary on my picci picci (my little moped) to visit Stan and Mark. I was looking forward to the afternoon break.

Even though I had been through a lot of violence so far to date, what was to happen that afternoon was going to have a serious impact on my life for the next twenty years.

Three o'clock came and I was making my way to the main compound gates when I saw a crowd of people there. Someone came running towards me crying out "They are killing two men, they are killing two men." I froze for a split second and felt like running in the other direction, but they were killing two men. Who was killing what two men and why?

This, for sure, was out of my experience so far, but I had to try and do something. I had always imagined that I would be quite heroic in some circumstances. Up till then Mary and I had been relatively brave, but this was something very different.

Well, I left the picci picci to its own devices and ran into the crowd. The crowd was big enough, they were made up of local villagers, some of whom I recognised, and most likely there were some passers by, too; there were 30 to 40 people in all. The villagers were holding sticks, using them as canes and whips. Their faces were a-glee with manic delight and they were screaming and wildly shouting something in the local Acholi language.

In the middle of this mass of people was an open-backed army jeep. My eyes fell onto the jeep's cargo. Two men were hog tied and on their knees in the back. The men were stripped to their waists and their skin was being whipped into discolouration and broken into a bloody wounded mess by the villagers. I could not believe my eyes, my brain could not connect that this was happening; murder was happening before my very eyes. I moved around the jeep and found three soldiers whipping the men into senselessness.

They reminded me of crocodiles with bait. There was blood, sweat and this desire for the KILL in the air. I started to scream at the soldiers to stop, stop this awful thing. I was just screaming into the face of one of the soldiers "NO NO NO!"

I looked behind me and inside in the compound I saw one of the Verona Sisters walking towards the crowd with puzzlement on her face. I ran out of the mob and grabbed her, as I knew she knew the local language fluently. Both of us ran into the crowd again. I was standing directly beside the jeep when I saw the first man collapse and not move again. His head was bloodied and smashed. The red blood was in stark contrast to his black tight curled hair.

I screamed at the soldier beside me to stop hitting the last man who was still on his knees. I reached out and touched his arm to try and get him to drop his weapon. It was then that evil burned into my eyes. His face was full of uncontrolled mania, lust and death, his face was splattered with blood which was not his, mingled with his own sweat. He brought up his two hands in the air, holding in one hand a whip and the other a large thick chain. He brought his face closer to mine and I felt he could have bitten my face off and eaten it raw because ANIMAL was written all over it, he wanted to hurt and consume something. He spoke to me and said, "If you don't shut up you will be next." Then he brought down the whip onto my back and laughed.

I remember not breathing and then the only thing that seemed to be alive and moving was my eyes. With all the will power I could find there was no way I could move. I was totally paralysed and had no control. Everything went strange. There was total silence, mouths were moving but no sound was heard anywhere. Everything went into slow motion, and I mean very slow motion, and I could not move.

My eyes were focused now on the kneeling man's head. Neither of our pairs of eyes flinched, they stayed wide open as I saw the damage the chain did in splitting his head wide open, blood splattered everywhere. My eyes saw that my yellow tee-shirt with a yellow rose on it was now red. We locked eyes again. This is all I knew I could give this man; blows came hammering down on him and the villagers kept whipping him, but neither he nor I flinched.

I remember trying to move my arms to get out my handkerchief to wipe the blood and brains from his face, but I could not move. Nothing seemed to matter any more bar keeping our eyes locked in as much love that I could give. It seems pathetic, but that was all I could do. The man began to wobble and was sitting now on his heels. Oh God, his face was a mess, ripped open, blood streaming down and now so much blood that it was hard for him to keep his eyes open. He started to fall to the side, when a soldier got into the cab and started to drive away. We kept looking at each other till he fell, still in the back, and the jeep drove away. I felt somehow attached and felt I was going with him. In the distance the jeep stopped again, where I found out later they finished him off.

I stood there just staring, then I bent over, coughing and wheezing, trying to make some noise, but nothing but wheezing came out. I looked around to see the very old Verona Father priest standing shouting at all the villagers that this was sin and he would never give any of them communion again. I just kept staring at the whole area as all the villagers seemed to disappear. I walked over to the priest and asked,

"WHY?"

He said that these two men were just walking the road, but were of Idi Amin's tribe, so they were killed. I just stood there in disbelief till there was no one left. I turned and I saw my picci picci still there, waiting for me to go to visit my friends. I did not know

47

what to do. Mary was busy teaching so I walked a mile down the road to visit the Verona sisters who were teaching in the local school. There was an outdoor play on and I watched that for a moment, wondering why I felt I was in a space suit and I was bobbing around this planet.

I walked into the convent and met Sr Catherine. I sat and told her the story. I desperately wanted to feel something. I thought I should feel something. I wanted to cry; I wanted to cry, but I heard myself repeating the same story in a detached emotionless way. I desperately wanted to feel or cry, but felt trapped in this "space bubble". Catherine made me repeat the story every time someone else came into the room, but I just seemed to be in this trapped emotionless state.

I went home and listened to the Italian doctors talk about the event and mention who was there: the priest, the nun and the villagers. They didn't mention me, so maybe I wasn't there, because I didn't feel anything; no outrage, fear, anything. I only kept seeing his eyes, those poor eyes and my inability to move. What a coward I was.

I replayed the event over and over in my head, each time changing the ending. I imagined that I jumped up on the jeep, told the soldiers to get lost and dragged the man off the jeep into the safety of the mission compound. Why did I not do that? The films would do that, why did I not? I tortured myself with this image. I then thought of Veronica wiping the face of Christ. I could not even do that, I could not move to even reach my handkerchief.

With reflection I saw the character and story of Veronica in a very new light. Veronica was in a crowd of people looking for a killing, too; there were soldiers there, too, who had whipped Christ to shreds. How brave, I thought now, that Veronica stood out of the crowd, fearless with a great act of compassion, letting Him know that he was not alone and even the smallest act of love was still alive in this brutal moment. She wiped that sorry face, mercy met mercy in that union of pain and then Veronica had to let him go.

Many of the stories in the bible became real for me, it became a living bible being repeated before my eyes. I still could not feel.

The next day we, the VMMs, had a mass. Again I told the story in an emotionless state. I never cried and felt so lost to myself that I became alien. That was the last time I gave any thought or remembered reflection to the incident. I was trapped, so I got on with life like everyone else and tackled new encounters with violence that only post war countries can know.

My life started to take on a very different direction. I ended up in the chapel more frequently. Doing that gave the only sense of order or meaning to what was going on in this beautiful country. Whenever I went to Kampala I stayed with The Franciscan Missionary Sisters For Africa who were doing extraordinary work with the casualties of violence and warfare. They were like the local hotel for everyone to go to stay with and be fed. We knew we would be reasonably safe there; well, for some reason I always felt safe there. With my new found interest in prayer I ended up joining the sisters on these occasion for mass and Benediction's, enjoying my visits there and finding their humour infectious.

One day Brendan was going to Kampala with two others. I joined him, as I thought I could stay with the sisters and do some shopping. We decided to leave Gulu early so as to make most of the day in Kampala. We sped off down the main road and then, out of the blue, there was an awful noise and soldiers everywhere jumping out of the ditches at us. They were pointing their guns and I knew that if Brendan didn't stop, we would all be shot. Suddenly we screeched to a dramatic stop. My door was opening and I was being forcibly dragged out the car by my hair. The next thing I was pinned down, spread-eagled on the bonnet of the car with something cold at my head. I wondered if I saw a dead body in the ditch.

The next thing I knew was that we were all in the car travelling in silence to Kampala. I was not sure what happened to them or me. All I knew was we were all OK now and we had shopping to do. We arrived at the Franciscans and were having a cup of tea when Brendan started to tell of what happened on the road. Another doctor/ sister came in at that moment and took on the conversation, telling us of her hard night in the hospital. Brendan stopped talking and we all never mentioned the incident again.

Most of us had some hijacking stories to tell but my story was hijacked, not hijacked? I am not sure!

One day I was travelling back from Kampala with the two Corti doctors and an old Italian Brother. He wore a white cassock and had a long, long white beard and looked quite emaciated; in fact he was as healthy as an old mule. We were travelling along a quiet part of the road when low and behold soldiers came out onto the road and made us stop the car. As we were stopping, Corti said to the old brother, "Lie down, pretend you are very sick and can't move." He did as he was told, we were all taken out at gunpoint and Corti started arguing and pleading with the soldiers that the old man was dying and he would die on the road if they took our car. I stood there and laughed to myself saying, this man has style! The soldiers were poking and shoving the old brother, but he lay there "dying". He could have won an Oscar for the show he was putting on and I was surprised that the soldiers did not turn round and slap us all.

The next thing we all saw in the distance a jeep coming along the same road. The soldiers ordered us all back in the Combi, saying they would take this jeep coming. It was then I felt bad and more than sorry for the poor sods behind us. The old priest sat up, patted himself down and we all travelled home safely, half smiling, half very upset for that car behind.

This was Uganda under Obote. Fuel was very hard to find as was everything else, but we VMMs decided we needed a holiday and had been saving fuel in the jerry cans. Stan and Mark thought it would be lovely to go camping in the Ruwenzori game park as we had actually met and liked the head game keeper there. He had said it was OK to go there, but just to make sure we arrive in the light and get to the "Bridge" before dark as the soldiers can cause trouble in the dark. They had thrown many a person over the bridge to the crocodiles. I was not sure on the name of the bridge but we knew it was by the entrance to the game park where the gamekeeper lived.

We decided to give it a bash, but we needed transport. I had the job of asking for a loan of an ambulance for our holiday. Our request was granted as we never used it up north as it was too dangerous. Off we went. We had collected as many tins of things, bread, beans and, yes, two crates of home brew. Mary and I had been on a roll!

The first night we went as far as Kampala, then headed further south to Ruwenzori. The sisters thought we were crazy, foolish and mad to do such a thing. We all just wanted a break. Off we went in our ambulance with Stan and Mark taking turns at driving. We had a few hitches on the way, taking the wrong turns, but we kept going and felt we were nearly there.

It was leaving 6.30pm and we had not reached this famous bridge yet; in 30 minutes it would be dark. Well, as Murphy's Law would have it we arrived bang on the bridge at 7 o'clock in perfect time for the darkness and perfect time for the soldiers. God, there they were, shit, we were crocodile meat! As usual they marched us out of the ambulance at gun point. They told us to put up our hands and marched us half way across the bloody notorious bridge where they lined us up. There we were, Scots and Brits alike, looking like complete cowboys with AK47s pointing at us.

I wanted to laugh uncontrollably as I thought we all looked ridiculous. One soldier pointed at Stan and took him away. It was a long walk. The headlights of our ambulance were still on and we all just stared until we could not see Stan anymore. All there was was silence and us standing in the headlights' glare with our hands still held high.

The next thing is that they came and took me away in the other direction. There were two of them, pointing their guns at my back leading me to the back of the ambulance. They ordered me into the ambulance and one of them got in with me. The next second, he just started looking around the ambulance for food. I thought "bugger", this is months of saving food, petrol and beer. At that moment I just thought he can do anything and take anything, but I won't let him take the beer. I had slipped the beer underneath the ambulance seats so I moved myself over there to distract attention and tell him where the bread was. He was delighted and took our whole supply plus as many tins as he could carry.

Simply enough they escorted me back to the line up where I saw Stan being frogmarched back. We were all then allowed to go and continue our journey. We continued for about 5 minutes in silence when I eventually said, "They didn't get the beer." We just burst out sniggering and laughing with delight. We may starve on this holiday, but we will still drink. Stan never spoke about what happened to him. We all never really referred to it again.

We had a great camping holiday. Every day we went into the lake and fished for our own food. We had a conveyer belt to behead, skin, fillet and cook the fish. It worked. We had plenty of corn and rice, so we filled up on that. One night we were sleeping. There were 4 in our tent and Stan and Mark in the other. We were woken by this horrendous roar, it went again and all I heard someone say was it is a rhino. I thought if it's a rhino we are dead, the nuns were right, we were mad to go on holiday! The beast was very close to us and the next thing we heard was the earth vibrate beneath us and this echoing loud roar. Oh God, we were done for as we all heard the stomping on the ground and it was so close. We all started telling each other to shut up in the hope that if we were quiet it might not see us!

We lay there like four sardines waiting to be squashed. The earth shook and the beast was charging, I didn't think we were going to survive this. Imagine, after all we had all been through, only to be killed while camping. The vibrations were rattling my ear drums and then suddenly the pounding was going past us and not through. We heard this enormous splash and all realised that it was a hippo. We thought "Hippos are not meant to be dangerous", but realised that if you are between it and the water you become the enemy. We were being warned! Eventually the four of us girls started sniggering uncontrollably and Margaret was desperate for a cup of tea. We all had to go for a wee, too, but were too frightened to go far.

Stan and Mark (our heroes) were camped behind the ambulance and called out were we OK? We snorted and sniggered "we're fine, just don't come out, we're not using our latrine!" We survived another tale. We packed up and moved away from that wonderful time in the game park and slowly made our way back up the west coast of Uganda and on to the Murchison Falls.

One night during our travels we had to cross the Nile. It was dusk and we drove the ambulance onto a pontoon. What a truly awesome experience to cross the Nile at night. It was so beautiful and so peaceful. The Nile is a wondrous and spectacular experience. That night was a night with the full moon and as we were crossing the Nile with the full moon shining, I thought of my mum and home. We had always said that if letters did not arrive then every time there is a full moon we will know that each of us is thinking of the other.

It was a peaceful journey and the next day we were told we could hire a boat to take us up the Nile. We thought that would be great and we scraped together enough cash for the venture. We were told when we arrived they had no petrol and if we could supply the petrol then the journey was on. Stan and Mark went back to the ambulance and calculated how much fuel was left and how much we needed to get home safely. Bingo, we had enough and went on a journey of a lifetime up the Nile to the Murchison Falls. There were definitely perks in being a missionary, you see things so extraordinary and in extraordinary circumstances. Hippos and crocs were everywhere. Many hippo had been killed for meat, but there were still enough to see.

We arrived back safely and life chundered on, working, teaching and listening to the news. You become creative when the lights go out and there is no electricity for days. Songs, poetry, stories are all told in abundance. There is a real bonding. During this time my two sisters came out to us for a holiday. I was looking forward to seeing them, but when they came off the plane they were terrified. They had been speaking to a BBC correspondent about going to Uganda for a holiday. They said that he looked horrified as didn't they know there were war-like conditions in the country?

Their plane was late and Brendan had had to go, so I had to take local transport back into Kampala with them. Of course there were check points, easy enough to negotiate, but I could see my two sisters ogled-eyed with fear. I really did not know why they were worried because it was only a simple check point.

We eventually got up to the Franciscan Hotel/convent. One of my sisters just started to cry when she heard the bombs and guns go off. I, in fact, just hadn't heard them. We sent her to bed and my other sister tackled me, saying "Tell the truth, how bad is the bombing?" To me there was no big deal and at that moment I really felt alien to their experience and a little lost as to what they were feeling. I packed her off to bed too.

The next day we had a ride up to Gulu in a jeep. There was a nasty moment when we were held up at a check point for a couple of hours, but were eventually let go to travel the rest of our journey. The food was a culture shock for my sisters and I really hadn't realised how much our taste buds had changed. I only prayed that there would be no shooting or looting in the village when they were here.

Their time went and they enjoyed going to the local market, and the girls and some locals had meals for them. They were valiant. Brendan had organised for us all to go to Kenya for a few days when saying goodbye to my two sisters, so off we went to Kampala where I needed to get cholera injections up to date. Clare and Frances stayed in town. At that time there was a gun battle down on the main street. Mary and I hadn't heard it and wandered back to my sisters. Clare had been terribly shocked by it all. Mary and I hardly registered the event, I don't know why, but things like that did not bother us any more.

Well, we made it to Kenya and said a fond farewell to Frances and Clare. I was thrilled that they came out and would be able to share in my story more, when I came home. We stayed in Nairobi for two days and had a ball. We bought tea mugs and all sorts of food seasonings, we were in heaven. In the hotel we stayed in we took a chance of phoning up room service and asking for a Coke. We had never had Coke or any beverage like that in all our time in Uganda. The man said back to us, "Sorry madam, we have no Coke, only Pepsi." Well, we rolled about the place laughing at the selection we had just been given. That became a little pet phrase of ours when things got tough, "Oh no, we only have Pepsi."

Both Mark and myself came down with a very nasty Hepatitis A. Both of us reckoned we got it on our Ruwenzori holiday. Mark went home and I was hospitalised for a while. It took me a couple of months to get back on my feet again and realise that my two years in Uganda was nearly up. What was I going to do? I had decided to join the Franciscan Missionary Sisters for Africa. I loved being a missionary, they were different "creatures" from ordinary nuns. I wanted this to be my life.

It was time to go home. Five of us were flying out on the same plane. There were four nuns and me. I was going to the airport early with Evert, the others would follow later on. It was a sinister journey along the Entebbe road as the previous week a Fr Bilbou had been shot in his car in a car-jacking. Thank God we arrived safely and I let Evert get back to the city. I waited on the other four nuns; I waited and waited. The plane was boarding and there was no sign of them; the plane took off without them and, as I was to find out later, they had left the convent about 15 minutes behind us to make sure they arrived on time too. They were all hijacked and left alive, but stranded, with nothing bar the clothes they wore. What an end to my sojourn in Uganda.

ETHIOPIA

I was so excited to be arriving in London; my two sisters had driven down to collect me as my home bound plane ticket did not include an onward flight to Edinburgh. It was fantastically wonderful to be back, but I felt so different, everything about me had kind of changed, but I couldn't put my finger on it. It was wonderful to see my mum and Nana and brother, but my heart was lost to Africa and what was going on in it. I was so desperate to join the Franciscans and get back.

The following month I was over in Dublin having my interview and psychological assessment. The assessment took a couple of hours and there was only one tricky moment when she asked me word association. She said "Axe", I said "Murder". I explained away the attack on the compound and Enrico guarding us in the bedroom with the axe. She didn't seem too impressed or interested in my time in Uganda and when I said "Tree" she moved on. I passed with no problem and before I knew it, it was July 17th, 1982, the day I entered the convent.

I cried for the first six weeks, I missed my G and Ts and wanted to meet up and talk with the Ugandan crowd, however they were all still out there and I had to put up with this. The postulancy ended and thankfully moved to Sandymount Dublin 4 where the novitiate was. There were only two of us and we spent a quiet two years learning how to pray, the history of the congregation, Franciscan lifestyle creative art and stuff like that. It was a tough two years and I learnt that I was quite angry, and even after a bit of therapy was never quite sure why.

I worked with the Simon community one afternoon a week and I enjoyed that. Later I was to work in the same kind of facility in Paisley, Scotland, for six months, they were times I enjoyed so much. I made my first profession and knew I needed to do midwifery if I was to go back out to Africa. I enrolled in Our Lady of Lourdes Hospital, Drogheda, and completed my two year midwifery diploma in1987.

I had been discerning with the sisters where I would go to next

Ethiopia: celebrating the feast of The Baptism of Our Lord and procession around the Church with The Holy Tabot

The Icon of Our Lady the Guardian at the entrance to our mission in Chencha

My mother on Christmas Day 1988 looking at the view from the
Chencha hills

Half way down our mountain, enjoying the view of Lake Abaya
and Chamo

An old lady carrying firewood while passing our mission compound

A TBA antenatal clinic

Ethiopia: the 15th century manuscripts in safe keeping in our kitchen cupboards

Mum and Annie holding the golden cross given by Haile Salasse

and with all the newspaper reports about famine and poverty in Ethiopia, I thought what better place for me to go. I had this drive to help, fix, heal. I suppose I should have known better.

My time now was to be spent trying learn about Ethiopia. It is unique and quite different from the rest of Africa. It is full of diversity because it is rich in every way possible, but I can honestly say that I had never seen such extreme poverty in all my life.

I arrived there early1987 ready to do anything but was immediately stopped in my tracks when I travelled out of the airport and bang into Red Square. It was how I imagined Moscow to be. Huge militaristic square with Marx, Lenin and Engles all over the place. Red Flags, red sickles and then I was told the history of The Red Terror.

Haile Salasi had been in power, he originated from a long dynasty of powerful Emperors. Salasi came to the throne in Ethiopia in 1930 and was killed by strangulation in the basement of his palace in 1975. Fifty nine members of the Royal family, ministers and generals were also executed around that time. It was a bloody coup by Haile Mengistu Mariam. His office was totalitarian style and the country's military was financed by USSR and Cuba. His ministry was called the Derg, thousands of suspected enemies of the Derg were tortured and killed.

Ethiopia easily slipped into communism during the late 70s and had a good hold of the people and land when I arrived in 87. The Ethiopian Orthodox Church, however, was deeply imbedded into the history and lives of the people there. They were allowed to function, but were always watched and life was made difficult for them. They had a rich tradition, claiming the Queen of Sheba as their own. Indeed, she is also known as the Queen of Ethiopia. They also claim its earliest origins from the Royal official said to have been baptised by Philip the evangelist (Acts8) and became an established church of the Ethiopian Axumite Kingdom.

There are 12 famous churches in Lalibella in the North of the country which have magnificent architecture and are known as the 8th wonder of the world. The Ethiopian church was a completely autonomous church. Many people thought it to be under the rule of

Egypt or Russia, but no, they had their own patriarch who was Abune Tekle Haymanot. He was no pushover and no friend of the Derg. He died when I was in Ethiopia in 1988, to be replaced by a very unpopular patriarch known to be more helpful to the Derg.

Ethiopia also claims to have the original "Ark of the Covenant" and no Ethiopian Church can be true and functioning without "a Tabot" in it, which is a replica of the Ark. Ethiopia is a mixture of Arabic type traditions and also Jewish in many ways. The Orthodox hold many of the same or similar dietary customs. There is no entry into the church for any woman having her menses and one must always remove the shoes while standing on holy ground. Indeed the Falasha Jews who descended from the house of Dan were living in the North of Ethiopia and were transported lock stock and barrel over to Israel in 1984, the movement ending in the 1990s.

Well, here I was in this vast country full of history and culture. It was an amazing land, where my passport was officially stamped in as 1980 Ethiopian time and 1987 the rest of the world time! Ethiopia still to this day lives off the Gregorian calendar, where most of the rest of the world lives off the Julian calendar. The official language of Ethiopia is Amharic and there are close to 275 letters in the alphabet. There are 13 months in the year and their new year is in September. They tell the time back to front, as many African countries do e.g. 8 o'clock is really 2 o'clock and 6 o'clock is really 12 o'clock. Their biggest feast days are not Christmas or Easter but Meskil, which is the finding of the true Cross and the Baptism of Our Lord.

I had to stay in Addis Ababa for a few days to get my travel documents in order and for the sisters to do a big shop. The first night there I saw food which is original and unique to Ethiopia. It is called Injera and Wat. It looked like grey cow stomach intestine lying flat out on a plate. The smell of the watt was indescribable too. In fact the Injera was made from fermented teff, then made into a large pancake and left for the week's rations. It is eaten cold and it took me a few months to get into liking the taste; once converted, however, I became a true believer and would eat it whenever I got the chance. The wat was the same. It was made of all sorts of vegetables, chicken or meat with spices galore and rancid butter put into the doro wat (chicken wat). I loved it, but it took a while as well to acquire a taste for the rancid butter.

Ethiopia was a country of spices. Everything was spiced and was tasty. I found it hard to sleep that first night in Addis Ababa as the altitude was about 8000 ft. Eventually we were ready to travel south making sure that we did not travel on Sundays. The communists had made that law, no movement or travel, I suppose to curtail people trying to go and worship. The journey was started as early as was possible. It would be a long day and I was told that it was a hard road to drive. We seemed to go for a couple of hours along one straight reasonable road, then we turned right along another long straight reasonable road for another 3-4 hours. We passed a beach called Langano which I was told was a nice place to have a break and where it was safe to swim, and just past Langano we stopped at Sheshamani to eat and have a break. It was a bit of a dive of a place but over the years I spent in Ethiopia grew fond of it and the food there, but that first day I picked and poked at the Injera. We turned right again as we continued our journey and now we hit a road that would not only rattle every bone in your body but would vibrate your teeth and eye balls. We may as well have driven over corrugated iron for 4 hours. I was totally rattled by the time we reached our next pit stop. Wolita Sodo, home of the hospitable Daughters Of Charity. They were kind as I found out they always were.

We had tea, then moved onto the last stage of my journey. We were heading for Arba Minch in the Gama Goffa region. There was our main house in Ethiopia. I was to stay there for a month or so to learn the language, but the last 3 hour drive to reach it was exhausting. One big cloud of dust the whole way and somehow it was all over the inside and outside of the car. I arrived like a red fireball. One of the sisters from Chencha, the mission I would end up in, had waited to see me and welcome me to Ethiopia. Most certainly everything about this land and mission was very different from my beloved Uganda, but I was totally mesmerized by it.

I settled in Arba Minch which means 40 springs and was amazed at the beauty around us. Sr Lena called it the A, B and C which

63

meant, Lake Abaya, the Bridge of God and Lake Chamo. I was told that the view from Chencha was breathtaking. I put my head down for the next six weeks to learn the Amharic; I had done a couple of weeks in Ireland before leaving so that stood me in good stead. I felt ready to travel to Chencha, the place of the poor.

Gamma Goffa was an amazing area. Although Amharic was the official language, there were 44 languages in this region alone. Everything about the country was unusual and very big, there were no small portions. Arba Minch was 2000ft above sea level, Chencha was 10000 feet above sea level, so it was a very cold place indeed. We would stop half way up the mountain to put on more clothes or if we were travelling down would strip off. We literally that day drove up and up right into the clouds. We ascended from the bottom of the mountain up a windy 12 mile path to reach our 10000ft heights. That day it only took about an hour and a half, but when Father Owen Lambert first made the climb in 1974 it took him nearly 7 hours, so progress had been made.

At one point in history Chencha had been the capital of Gammo Goffa, but as I heard later the only thing going for it was the high altitude with no mosquitoes. It was an extremely cold day up in Chencha, Arba Minch had been lovely and warm, but when I arrived to a happy reception I was welcomed into a house with a log fire roaring. There was no electricity on our compound and no hot water, although there was a bath with a gas cylinder attached when needed. There was a gas cylinder cooker but most of the cooking was done on a solid fuel fire and we always made sure we had a supply of dry wood in the house.

It was the wettest, dampest and most miserable climate I have ever lived or worked in. For eight months of the year there were just different levels of fog around. For about two of these months it was very dangerous indeed as you literally could not see in front of your nose.

Maureen, Aine and Paula were the sisters I would be living with, nurses/midwives, and I had a lot to learn. There were two Spiritan men (Holy Ghost) there, too, one was Fr Emmanuel Fritz, a French Byzantine priest, and Br Dennis. He was a quiet man, but an inspiration. The translation of Dennis was "dull one" so Dennis was known by the locals as "Tadu" which meant "Renewed". If there was one thing to say about him and that would be his genuine love of the poor and the poor loved him. Dennis acted as a social worker. He would look into the cases of the really poor and destitute, take them to the hospital when needed, build small houses for them and make sure they had blankets for the real cold nights. Ethiopia's young people had disappeared which left a lot of destitute old. There had been a war going on with Eritrea in the north for years and at certain times throughout the year, the communists would do night time raids, ripping away 14, 15 and 16 year old boys. They would be gathered in a huge field outside Chencha town and starved for days. They were only fed alcohol so eventually they were literally shipped out, blind drunk, taken as bullet fodder to the north. Most families never saw their young boys again. It was a horrendous event waiting to happen every year.

Well, I had arrived safely and was settling in to my new environment. I really felt the altitude get to me for the first three weeks or so. Every thing up here was so different from everything down there in Arba Minch. I often felt like Jack in the Bean stalk, we really were in a different world. Fr Emmanuel was a Byzantine priest and it had been decided long ago that we would not be making a Roman Catholic presence as such, but join the Orthodox in their worship; Emmanuel was to help establish a training school for Orthodox Deacons and priests. They were in dire need of assistance to help them explore their rich heritage. Emmanuel could not officially do any Church work in this communist land, so had to take the job of water worker, well digger, supplier of clean water to clinics. It was a job badly needed and fair dues to him, as an academic guy he took this role on gallantly.

We had a small chapel just outside our convent and it had a full orthodox flavour, but on Sundays we joined the Ethiopian Church for prayer and mass. It was an eye opener, I felt I was going back in time to the very time of Jesus. At times you nearly could hear a director call out "roll them cameras", it all seemed so surreal.

A typical Sunday would be up at 5am, have a cup of coffee then head off together to the Church. All Ethiopian Churches, if possible, are built on a hill or mountain, ours was on a small hill a bout two miles away from the mission. Outside the fence of the Church you would have the "unworthy/unclean" there. They would beg from you and you were meant to give them something because by doing that you would receive a blessing from God. There would be others inside the gate of the Church compound, then others outside the doors of the Church. The closer you got to the holy of holies, which was inside the centre of the Church the more worthy you were. Everyone, without exception took their shoes off and left them outside the Church. You then kissed the lintels of the church door, stepped inside and kissed the floor. There were a couple of curtains that you could go through if you thought you were worthy and then you would be standing near to the Holy of Holies, men on one side and women on the other.

The Ethiopian nuns would be there, too. They were usually grandmothers who were now widowed and helped to serve the church, as Anna in the bible did. Again, an ancient rite. Once settled in, a prayer stick was thrust at you and you would be more that happy to use it. A prayer stick was used to prop you up during the long service. The mass would take three to four hours every week and there was no sitting allowed. The stick was long and you dug it into the earth and propped the handle under you chin and leant against it to give yourselves rest. The religious language was called G e ez. Emmanuel was learning it. The Ethiopian priests, who were married, made three breads the night before in a small room, called the Bethlehem, beside the Church. Usually in the Bethlehem there were three ostrich eggs as a sign of fertility. The breads were called holy bread. One of these breads would be picked the next day during the mass to consecrate, the other two would be eaten or broken up and sent to the sick.

The priests would come into the holy of holies where much of the activity took place (we could not see the goings on through the shut doors.) There would be three, first reading a psalm and then eventually the Gospel. Everyone in the congregation was to kiss the book of life before being read. The singing that was done throughout was very Indian sounding and it is a very specialised practised intonation.

Eventually communion would come. Most folk did not go, but the ones who did were babies and old people. Only these groups of people were deemed innocent. It was a rich service. The babies would be fed the wine on a holy spoon. They lapped it up then were latched onto the mother's breast. Adults went up and opened their mouths. A piece if bread (like rolled up dough) was dropped in, then a spoon of wine, then a handful of blessed water to wash it all down. After that was the sermon, which could go on for at least an hour; after that every psalm in the bible had to be said. Usually what happened there was every Deacon was given a first line of the psalm, they all may be prompted to say four or five psalms each so the 50 odd psalms would be said at once. It sounded very like a charismatic speaking in tongues prayer group.

After that everyone had to stay for the blessing of the priest and individually we had to "kiss his holy hand full of Mercy and compassion." It was usually 10 o'clock before we were out, often covered in lice.

Lice, fleas, bed-bugs and rats were the definite negatives about living in Chencha. They were not the occasional thing but a lived, every day thing. Life was hard and very, very cold up there. Firewood was hard to come by for the people, so it was very difficult to be washed every day! I understood the poverty of the fleas and lice. The rats truly were a plague, we did everything to get rid of them, but they were an on-going problem, as many a visitor would testify to.

We had 39 clinics all over the mountain range. We did mother and child health care and also worked in antenatal care with the TBAs. They were the Traditional Birth Attendants. These were ordinary women from each village who were naturally called by the people to help the women deliver in their villages. They had a natural talent for midwifery. They were all illiterate and had their own jobs in the market or digging food for the family. Each year they would be gathered together for a seminar and build on their skills. It was slow, but the simpler it was kept, the more efficient the whole thing ran.

The sisters who had started this mission in the 70s had established this as a role model for many an area of work. There were 39 outstations, three nurse midwife sisters and three to four trained health assistants. Over the years, people who had worked with the mission were sent for further training within Ethiopia, all this took time in a communist country. Nothing was easily established.

Every day there were one or two clinics on around the mountain. At certain times of the year we were able to avail of the land rover, at other times, well most times during the year, it was either walk to work or take a mule. Maureen was known to often take a mule to work. I had tried it and decided that a walk would be better for me. The distance to the clinics varied, the shortest walk was 1 ½ hours, the longest 3 hours, we'd do the clinic and then walk back. It was a great opportunity to spend time in the villages with the people and hear their stories.

It was also a great time to meet and discuss cases with the TBA. They had often picked out someone whom they were worried about and we would discuss what treatment or care would be needed. Simple things saved lives, like if the TBA knew that if the "Belly" was so big and the head was still at the side of the belly, well, this lady needed to come to us at the mission. The woman would be referred to the hospital in Arba Minch and hopefully deliver safely there.

I was always amazed at the strength of the Ethiopian women. Many who lived mountains away and had no effective health care walked 2-3 days over the mountain range with a ruptured uterus. We would have died immediately, but often they survived. Part of our job was to take them up and down the mountain. In reality we were all an unofficial ambulance service. Many a severe headache we all got belting up and down the mountain so fast.

Awful things still happened. One day I was walking back from a clinic with the team over a muddy field. It was lashing with rain and in the middle of the field I saw a crowd of women all with their shawls raised so as to cover something on the ground. They started to shout at me to come over. I ran over, got on my knees and put my head under the igloo of shawls to see a woman bleeding badly, on her back with a dead child still attached to the placenta and the placenta still attached to the mother. There was blood, mud, rain and mess all over. The placenta needed to come out and quickly, too. I did a manoeuvre I'd seen before and managed to remove the placenta intact. Immediately her uterus contracted and thankfully the bleeding stopped.

At that point the people picked the woman up and carried her to the roadside. It was pouring and as I looked down, the dead baby was all alone, left and forgotten in the mud. It was a melancholic moment. I just spat on my finger and baptised the child, I only had an old maize sack in my rucksack, so wrapped the child in that and ran after the family, who were just so relieved that the woman was not dead that they forgot the baby. It was a terrible sight that day. I gave the mother some antibiotics to take and told her to see Dr Fitzum in the local Chencha hospital. They left and I was covered in mud, blood and sadness.

Another day, walking back from clinic, another group of women shouted to us. There was a woman lying at the side of a ditch who had literally bled to death there. It was a dreadful sight to see and there was nothing to be done bar we all knelt and said a prayer and continued our walk home. Another day a woman had arrived at our compound in a bad way. She had walked for a day and a half over the mountains in bad labour. We had no transport that day so we walked over to Dr Fitzum, about a mile away. The baby was dead and her uterus not yet ruptured and the woman was fully dilated but with a brow presentation. That meant the baby was stuck. Together we had to do a craniotomy there and then. The baby had obviously been dead for a few days and the mother exhausted but alive.

The mother and child clinics were very busy. We had immunizations all over the mountain. We did that in conjunction with the government hospital. There were a few little communist spies in that group so we always had to mind our Ps and Qs. There was a Gaelic saying we all came out with if we thought one of us was talking too much about anything in front of the spies. Most of our movements would be reported and if we visited anybody just "willie nilly" then that person would be interrogated by the "gwadenyas". Indeed it was known that our night watchman was regularly reporting on what we were doing in the compound. When he died we were able to hire someone more accommodating to us.

Our mother and child clinics were busy with vaccination programmes and pneumonia, malnutrition, worms, vomiting, and diahorea and scabies. We treated all these things and gave lectures every clinic on hygiene and a balanced diet. We gave out a high protein powder called "faffa" to the malnourished and kept the height for weight charts up to date. There was a terrible Vitamin A deficiency and we saw many a melted cornea due to this. We decided to give the mothers a good dose of Vitamin A antenatal which would help the child over the first few months of life.

On one of our clinics in Dorze, (half way down the mountain) we were in the middle of a mother and child clinic when we heard this awful commotion outside. People were carrying in a young lad who seemed to be bleeding all over his face and hands. The people explained that this boy was a farmer and he was digging his land when they found a strange looking stone. This boy was looking at the stone when it blew up. Of course we realised it was a grenade. The boy looked awful, his eyes were blown out of his face and it looked like one hand was blown off. I said we would need Intravenous fluids on him before travelling down the mountain, and hoped the government hospital might have some in store. I got into the jeep with the lad, and the father asked if he could join us.

I was delighted the family member could be with us and as we drove off in the jeep, bouncing along the rough road, the dad said he just did not understand how a stone could blow up. But to prove it he brought another one to show us, as he proudly stuck an old grenade under my nose. Paula and I both screamed for the car to stop and explained to the man that this stone, too, could blow up if he did not hold it carefully. We asked him to get out of the car and walk up to the police station where we would meet him.

We took the lad to the hospital, then told the police that the father was going to appear soon with an old grenade. The police were great and they met the father and threw the grenade down a latrine! Hopefully it exploded down there. The boy was taken to Arba Minch where it was confirmed he lost the sight of both his eyes and the use of one hand. We were told that occasionally people still found grenades and bullets left by the Italians in 1941, when they had a brief occupation of the land. How sad that old military equipment was still able to destroy lives.

SOWING SEEDS IN ETHIOPIA

We never knew what each day would bring under the communist regime. This kind of system slowly eats away at your soul. Everyone had to be the same, get the same, act the same. There was no initiative allowed, creativity died and every hope and dream was banished by the system. One thing is sure, the poor got poorer and there was equality and equality?! The head of the communist party in Chencha was a fair man who was not a bully and did not make life intolerable for the people or us, but he was still a communist having to do his job. We were watched ok and our mail at times was censored. Magazines and papers did not always come through when there were sensitive things happening in USSR or Ethiopia, but mostly we went about our business with happy caution. Naïve, you could not be, as this could put people's lives at risk. I always felt a terrible oppression in that country during that time

There was a poverty in Ethiopia which is hard to explain. Half way down the mountain there was a village called Ochollo. It was an outcast village. The potters lived there. Potters were "dirty" people and you could not associate with them They lived in the worst part of the mountain. It was full of caves and the caves full of hyrax rats. The hyrax rat was host to the sand fly and the sand fly bit the people and gave them a rare disease with no known cure called Lieshmanisis. This disease affects both the liver and the skin. They were an outcast people, who really looked the part, their skin was covered in sores and they were as poor as mice; I would also say the mice in Ochollo had more riches than them. The other diseases affecting them were elephantitis and relapsing fever.

These potters were also allowed to be "carriers". This meant that the women could go to the bottom of the mountain and compete with the donkeys and occasional taxi to carry "loads" up the mountain. The women potters were cheaper to hire than the donkeys so they got good custom. They had a 12 mile hike up that mountain with loads that could weigh30-40 kg. I had tried to lift one of the loads one day and could not budge it. It was a harrowing sight to see and that is how they made their money. We had food clinics there, as well as the mother and child and antenatal clinics. One woman who usually came to the food clinic was very ill. We climbed around the mountain to bring her food and a blanket. Her house was made of bamboo, it was five foot high and about the same in length. There was nothing in it bar a mat to lie on and three stones to put her pot on. Words will never be able to express the feelings you get when facing such stark poverty. It was people like that whom Dennis worked with and helped. I always took my hat off to him.

The houses around the Chencha area, but especially Dorze people, were quite unique. They were made of bamboo and in the shape of a beehive. They were very impressive to see. It was even more impressive to see them moving house. You needed at least 10 – 15 men who stood inside the structure. They dug up the bamboo foundations, then with a unique technique lifted the whole house up from the inside and then walked with the house to wherever you were told you were to move. All someone would see was this huge house move towards you and 20-40 shuffling feet.

Often the communists would just come along and tell villages to move. It was awful. People had grown their "inset", which is their false banana and main source of food, all around their house. It takes 7 years for the "inset" to be ready to eat. The communists may tell them they have to move by next week 7 miles away! No wonder there was famine.

The Dorze people were also quite unique on the mountain, as the men rode horses and wore these extremely baggy, colourful, woollen woven trousers. They wore matching woollen hats, too, of bright yellow, red and black. They were quite a sight on their steeds.

Every Saturday when we had all finished our morning work Dennis gathered everyone together on the compound to have a coffee ceremony to finish the week. The coffee ceremony in Ethiopia is nearly a religious ceremony, it is so full of welcome and ritual. The coffee we drank was the poor man's coffee. We would collect the coffee leaf and put it into a pot to boil along with onion, garlic, pepper, chilli pepper, ginger, rosemary, sage, thyme, salt and coriander. It was quite a concoction and would and could clear up any nasal congestion anyone was suffering from. We would all sit around in a circle and say a small prayer of coming together, then the coffee was brought in and the small tray with the small cups. There were about 8 cups and at least 12 people. Everyone shared the cups around and made sure everyone had at least three cups each. As we finished that, we all knew the work was done for the week and could go home.

There was another coffee ceremony which would happen in people's houses. The floor would be covered in fresh pulled grass. There would be incense burning and the coffee brought out by the woman of the house. Again you would have this coffee bean coffee, as Ethiopia is the Motherland of coffee. Rancid butter would be placed on top of the coffee and you would have to take at least three cups to show you enjoyed it and know you would be welcome back to the house. It was quite a trial until you got used to the rancid butter.

Another way I tasted coffee was in the desert with the nomads. They fried the coffee beans with the kernel of the bean still on, then melted oil and boiled fresh camel's milk. They had huge mugs to pour in the milk, add the oil on top and float the fried coffee beans (at least 10 of them) on top of. I remember looking at this concoction thinking "how on earth are you supposed to swallow this?" My friend Dina, who was American turned to me and said, "slurp up a couple of beans in your mouth, crunch them till you taste the taste of coffee and slurp up the milk through your teeth, swigging up some oil and swallow the lot!"

This I did and it was strangely pleasant!

Before I had arrived in Ethiopia, I had heard that the team in Chencha were opening up a new clinic. It was called Shama which means Light. People in Scotland gave me money for the Shama project and when I arrived I was to put the money to good use. Shama was a very difficult place to get to and Fr Emmanuel and his team had been working on making a road passable.

The team went in, there was to be a water well, social and health clinic. There were many meetings with the people there to see how they could help and be involved. The least we did the better for self reliance. The people could build the structure; all they needed from us were nails. They would make some bamboo furniture and if we could supply wooden tables and a few chairs it would be great. We would want them to pick a TBA who we could work with and we would also supply trees. The money from home would come in useful.

I thought I had nothing better to do than to buy tables and chairs, but lo and behold there were no shops that sold such things. Then I thought, "oh well, someone will make them." That was grand, but I had to supply the material. Wood and trees were under the authority of the communists and you needed lots of permission to get the same. Eventually Dennis helped me out because I was out of my depth. I had to buy a tree, get someone to chop it up, then hire mules to pull it up to the mission. Then I had to hire the carpenter to make the furniture. What a performance the whole thing was.

Eventually it was all made. The next problem was how to get it out to Shama. The roads were still bad and we could not use our transport yet. I waited till the weather was drier, tied all the stuff to the top of the land rover and set off. Half way into Shama we heard this awful crunch coming from the roof. We stopped immediately to find we had hit a low branch and all the legs of the tables had been broken off. I was so down cast and nearly ashamed at the whole performance to get this small project done and now when I arrive at the clinic it was all shattered. We drove on resolutely and when we arrived there was great celebration. Before I knew it, the tables and chairs were all fixed and suddenly functioning in this lovely new mud and wattle clinic.

Later we planted trees around Shama and loads of fruit trees, too, that the farmers might make some loving off. I also, with the aid of Fr Owen, planted thousands of Lucinda tree seedlings. There was awful soil erosion on the mountain which contributed to the malnutrition in the area. I thought if the soil erosion could be helped by tree planting, then we might be able to sow small vegetable gardens with carrots in them. At least this would help the vitamin A deficiency problem. Owen had discovered that the Lucinda tree would help the soil and if kept cut the trimmings could be fed to the cattle. Owen arrived with seeds to the house which were to be plunged into boiling water to start them off. I did that then took them down to the government's agriculture area, half way down the mountain. He had agreed to have these trees in the nursery there and when they were viable seedlings disperse them to the farmers. It worked and the farmers were delighted. I did not stay long enough in Ethiopia to see if they made any long lasting help with the soil erosion.

Life was interesting and you had to be able to change with the needs of the people around you. I had been deeply disturbed by the awful blindness that I saw from untreated trachoma. One day when I was in the hospital in Arba Minch there was an advert up saying there was a course in eye diseases and treatment coming up. The course would be a week long and we would be spending most of it in bush clinics. I was thrilled and I put my name down for it. The person giving it was an ophthalmic consultant. I was the only nurse at it, the others were all health assistants. I was hooked.

I walked into a whole new world. Anyone who specializes in eyes will understand what I mean. More than anything else, eyes seem to have a life of their own. I learnt a huge amount the first day about blindness, trachoma and Vitamin A deficiency. The next four days we were in the field being taught how to do Tarsal lid rotations. The health assistants were expert, it was unbelievable what they did. Chronic trachoma leads to scarring in the inside of the eyelid. The scarring causes the eye lid to shrink, retract, causing the eyelashes to point into the eyeball instead of outward. With the tarsal lid rotation, you would numb the eyelid, flip it open, cut the upper lid and detach some of the muscle and stitch it up again. All of a sudden the eyelashes were pointing in the right direction again, thus preventing the eyelashes scratching the cornea and causing blindness. This operation could be done anywhere.

It was a brilliant course and when I went back to Chencha I continued our normal clinics while educating about eye diseases. I worked with Dr Fitzum doing tarsal lid rotations. He was so interested himself that he took over the work and I believe went on to do an ophthalmic course himself. I continued my interest in "eyes" and went to ALERT Hospital in Addis Ababa (which, by the way, means new flower) and worked under an Egyptian ophthalmic surgeon for six weeks learning and learning. When I came back, I left Fitzum doing the operations and I went out to the primary schools to do a six week eye check and treat the trachoma and hopefully prevent the long term complications of blindness.

My mother came out to visit me for 6 weeks and she too was enthralled by the heritage of the land and saddened by the utter poverty of it.

We did some of the usual things you do with someone visiting and that was to visit the museum. It was there we saw "LUCY". Lucy had lived more than 3 million years ago and is supposed to be the oldest body found. It was all very interesting and it was great to have Mum up the mountain with us. We continued our work and Mum just joined us.

One day we went to visit some of the priests and Ethiopian nuns at a Marian shrine. Of course the Church was up a high mountain and very difficult to get to. We were invited to drink the local brew and then we were taken into a house of treasures. There was a bamboo hut at the side of the Church. It was full of umbrellas for the church service of Timket (the baptism of our Lord) hanging up. The colour was amazing. The next thing, the priest went over to what looked like our old kitchen cupboard from the convent (indeed it was, too.) In the cupboard were ancient manuscripts from the 12th, 13th and 14th century. Fr Emmanuel had seen them lying getting eaten by rats and eroded by dampness, so had volunteered our kitchen unit to help preserve the same. We were both overawed by seeing such rare beauty stuck in our old drawers! They then pulled out two huge Ethiopian crosses. One pure silver, one pure gold. They had been given them by Haile Selasi before he was murdered, and would be priceless in worth. We thanked the priests and nuns for their openness and hospitality to us.

Mum and I travelled all over the south of Ethiopia, spending time with the Hammer nomads in Dimika and seeing another mission territory in Jinka. A highlight must have been going on a boat trip to Lake Chamo to see some of the biggest crocodiles I had ever seen.

Neither of us will ever forget that trip. We arrived at the edge of the lake and for some reason had to go out to the boat in what was like an old bath tub. We really had to balance or we would have fallen in the water. The boat to take us out to the crocs was full of Ethiopians who were down at the hospital for a conference. I had never seen the boat so full and was immediately anxious.

We chugged out over the lake. It was full of huge Nile perch and catfish. We were blessed to have such delicious food around us. As we reached the place of the crocodiles everyone made a rush towards the left hand side of the boat and lo and behold the boat started tipping over. The captain just started yelling at everyone "Balance the boat, please balance the boat!" Everyone stopped in their tracks and realised we were in a very precarious situation, with hungry huge crocs only a hundred yards away. Well, we did as we were told and indeed we did balance the boat and all saw the crocodiles, and what is more we paid to have such an experience! We got back into our bath tub and eventually reached dry land. We knew we had had a close call.

As Mum was leaving the country there was a terrible meningitis epidemic outbreak. I was glad she was leaving; as yet we had no vaccines for ourselves or the people. Over 25,000 people had been known to be dead and the whole thing was spreading like wild fire. The government did not want to know about it and we had absolutely no supply of vaccine. We all took rifampicin as a hopeful preventative, but it was a scary place to be in. Mum went home and we picked up one vial with 50 doses in it. Some of the Daughters of Charity had this in their fridge so we took it back with us. All the mission personnel and the Ethiopian staff got vaccinated, but we all felt quite guilty.

Someone had been in Ethiopia and when they went home had been interviewed, they asked the WHO to help send out immediate supplies of vaccine to the area. The vaccine was sent but held up in the airport by the government of the time, claiming that only 20 people had died from a small outbreak. We had people all around us dying and we were impotent to get the vaccines down to us. Meanwhile the Holy Ghost fathers, MMM sisters and ourselves, set up famine tents to deal with the ill people and stop the hospitals being made useless due to over crowding. People were everywhere. Nails needed to be hammered into the trees to hang intravenous drips and antibiotics. Someone else drew up water into syringes, while someone mixed the medicine, while someone administered it, while someone else constantly kept up supplies of antibiotics and intravenous solution.

Eventually the ministry of health in Gammo Goffa realised there was a disaster happening before their eyes. The answer was 2,000 vaccines were sent down to us! It was impossible. The population of Ethiopia was 40-50 million, on Chencha mountain alone there was an estimated 87,000 people and we were given 2,000 vaccines. We were told that we were not allowed to administer any vaccine to any child, only adults, and the soldiers were to be there to see we followed orders.

That day was probably the worst day of my life. Mothers were flinging their babies at us to get the vaccine. They were crying "give the baby my vaccine." It was awful. The whole thing was awful. Tens of thousands appeared that day and we only had 2,000 vaccines. I felt like a Nazi: here, I give you life and here, go away, I can't give you life. I know many of these infants must not have survived. Something broke in me that day, but we were too busy with too many ill people to reflect on it.

I developed a small but very nasty tropical ulcer over that time. Antibiotics and salt packs worked fairly well.

Over one week later thousands of vaccines arrived. Every day we had one team who combed the mountain looking for any new outbreak. If we did then we would isolate them all and give treatment accordingly. We were very proud over that eight month period that we stopped the epidemic travelling up the mountain. We had a great system put in place and we did vaccinate multiples of thousands over that time. For me that was my lowest ebb in Ethiopia. It sapped the life out of me and I saw how evil and impossible it was to work in a communist country. Ideologies come first, then maybe people.

I knew I needed a break from the drudgery and dire solemn poverty of the whole place and situation. I decided to go to Debre Ziet, a small run Jesuit prayer centre, which had to be really portrayed as a holiday home as our next door neighbours were the Cubans who were rock solid communists. I took a two week break there. On my way I stopped off at Langano to wait for my friend Dina to arrive and we would have a break together. At Langano I met a South African white gold miner. He was telling me about the lucrative goldmines all around Ethiopia, he was nearly finished with his job and was soon to go home. He said that the gold went to the USSR in return for arms and munitions. I knew this was the case but meeting him was a sickening confirmation about the injustices that the ordinary Ethiopian was enduring.

Debre ziet was a God send and I got lost in so many novels and was able to swim in the wonderful crater lake just below the Jesuit centre. It was there on that holiday I had my first experience of "skinny dipping" and it was great. I went back depressed in myself still feeling something awful inside. All I wanted to do was cry and I did not know why. The year struggled on and I ended up with a dose of malaria, most likely from my holiday, and a bad dose of Giardi, which is a sort of nasty dysentery.

I had been training to go on a yearly pilgrimage called Elle Gabriel, but have felt too weak to do the hike. It is an amazing pilgrimage to Gabriel and one of the care assistants said that over 10,000 people go to it. The pilgrim has to leave Chencha on the Monday and walk over all the mountain range for the celebration on the Wednesday. It is a rough tough time seemingly and Maureen has done it a number of times. You walk all day and sleep rough over the next few days, too. By the time they all come back they are washed out with exhaustion, but they have prayed for all their intentions. It is quite something to be part of, even just watching them pass in their droves past the window.

Before I knew it I was due home for my home leave, the three years had gone by very quickly and although I had loved the country, I knew that I would not return. I was feeling terribly dead in myself and didn't know what to do; plus I was not feeling physically well.

FROM ASSISI TO TANZANIA TO KENYA

On my return home it was great to have my mum to talk to and understand the conditions that I had been living with. I was very angry at the shops in Edinburgh. They all seemed so pretentious and for some reason I vented my anger out on the shop called 'Evelyn and Crab Tree'. It just sickened me. I found all the choices too overwhelming for my brain and all I wanted to do was cry and cry. I did, till everyone was sick of me. I was just in awful pain and depression, I think, about such contrasts in life.

One day I was at the table with my sister and her friends when I just burst into tears because their conversation was so interesting and diverse. I realised out in Chencha, we talked about the walk to the clinic, what happened in the clinic and the walk back home. We were cut off from the world up there with no newspapers, TV, and radio was on and off. Suddenly I felt bombarded with information and choices, it was awful and I didn't think I was coping well at all.

Luckily I was given a chance to go to Assisi for a month's pilgrimage. It changed my life; it was the most wonderful time in my life and I was captured by the Franciscan and Clarisan Spirit of Assisi. I came home and fell ill. I needed hospital treatment and physical recuperation time. It was decided that I should stay home for a while. I became editor of The Congregation's magazine which was great fun and did mission appeal work. After that year I went to Canterbury and did my Diploma of Franciscan Spirituality. That is my most precious education certificate so far in my life. I loved the study and spirit, especially of St Clare of Assisi. She became part of my life and has helped me through my life thus far.

I was captivated by both these saints' stories, something was resonating in me but could not figure out what. Francis was a vain young man full of himself and his life story was about the emptying of the same. He had wanted to go to war and be a hero, but had been captured and imprisoned for a year by Assisi's enemy, Perugia. The horrors of war and his yearlong imprisonment must have changed him, but how? This I don't know, because after his father ransomed him out of jail, Francis was making plans to go back to war. In fact he did and reached a nearby valley were they were resting, when Francis heard a voice telling him to go home. He went home, but was never the same. It must have been shocking for his family and friends to have him come back and questions must have been rumoured all over Assisi as to what happened. Was he ill or just a coward? Francis withdrew. He withdrew from family, friends and social life, he withdrew up into the caves of Mount Subasio and stayed there for a year, alone, in darkness. Seemingly some scholars say that he was experiencing a nervous breakdown in that lonely dark place. We were shown in the writing s of Francis that during that time he was desperately looking for direction. After one year he came out of the cave and down a dusty mountain were he found a derelict church. There was a Cross hanging there which spoke to him. It simply said, "Francis repair my church which is falling into ruin." Francis had his mandate, the mandate he had spent a year in darkness listening for. At times I wondered what was my mandate, what was I listening for in my life. I did not know but I did know that the stories of Francis and Clare hit a deep place of wonder within me.

Throughout the three years at home something in my soul never recovered, but I was asked to go to Kenya for my next assignment. I said yes, but deep inside felt dead and something was constantly paining me. I dreaded saying goodbye to my family this time. It was such a heavy heart that I had, but I tried my best to be up beat.

I had just had a couple of tooth abscesses and eventually had two teeth out just before I flew out to Kenya. I spent one night in Kenya then was sent by plane to Tanzania to learn the language of Kenya which was Kiswahili. We arrived in the capital of Tanzania, Dar e salaam. It was a rough old place and that night some young street children set a fire ablaze underneath our bedroom. We were awake all night because of it, but we also had to be up by 4am to go to the airport and catch the plane up into the desert to a place called Kipalapala.

My gums were throbbing badly and the last place I wanted to land was the desert, in the middle of nowhere. When we eventually landed on a tiny grass strip we were met by the White Fathers who ran the language school. They had not expected us to come, they did not have our names and they said the classes were fully booked. That should have been an omen for me to get out of there, but like a good missionary asked was it possible to stay. All I knew at that point was that it was impossible to go.

I had brought money to pay for the course so it was decided that it was OK to stay. There were two of us doing the course. Pauline knew a fair bit of Swahili, I knew none. It was a nightmare. We were given one bucket of water a day and on Saturdays there was hot water. There was a young French Canadian girl who had never been in Africa before. It was a real culture shock for her not to have a washing machine and we had to teach her the basics of hand-washing! She had brought 21 pairs of underwear with her so when the 22nd day drew near we all geared up to watch the first attempt at hand-washing being done.

We had silly harmless fun. There was a sister there from Italy who had run in the Olympics, she was a fascinating character going out for her jog every day. Some of the young lads said one day they would go with her, well she took off and left them standing, they did not know what had hit them as they had not heard that she was an Olympic athlete.

My teeth became unbearably sore and I knew I was in trouble. If there were any real problems the local vet took care of things. If it was very serious then we had to go to hospital which was nearly half a day's journey away. There were no telephones around either. Well, one day I felt something sharp piercing my gums. I took my eyebrow plucker and attacked my gum. I pulled and poked till I eventually pulled out two bits of broken tooth left in my gum. I then packed my gums with salt and after a few days that problem healed up.

I had this constant pain inside me the whole time. I did not know why and I could not focus on anything, let alone being in the desert trying to learn a new language. The whole time was a night mare, I had pain, pain and more pain and spent all my energy trying to rise above it. The sister who was an Olympic athlete was also a therapist, so I had a few chats with her, which generally helped me through the three month ordeal in the desert.

During the Kiswahili course I realised that our visa for being in Tanzania was to expire three days before the end of the programme. We told the director and he was alright about it. There were three of us who needed to go early. With 6 weeks to go, the big news was that the "fire engine" was broken. I thought, "so what", but did not realise the full implications for us. The fire engine had been collecting wood in the forest and broke some important piece. That meant that no small aircraft could land or take off from the airport. Well, surely it would be fixed in six weeks time. Little did I know the speed of things in Tanzania.

The six weeks came and there was the fire engine, still broken with no sign whatsoever of being repaired. Tanzania at that time had one of the worst road or rail net work systems known. There were no buses or trains for at least another week and our visas were going to be out in a day or two. I was beginning to panic, but the director said that he had found a bus for us and it would take the three of us to Arusha were we could easily get a connection to Nairobi. That was great, but the bus did not show up the first or second day. Eventually he told us of another bus going the same direction.

There were a group of Tanzanian nuns who owned a bus. They bought it to transport their Superior around Tanzania and at the same time make room for about 30 more paying passengers. We had the money so we got the seats. It was great, one of the sisters had learnt to drive a bus and the other was a trained mechanic, it was a great system. We were about four hours into the journey when we heard an awful bang. The back wheel had blown open. We all lumbered out and sat on the sand. There was an awful lot of banging and clanging. This went on for over an hour when we were told the wheel was stuck on and they were going to have to try and hitch a lift back to Kipalapala to get the right tools to come back and fix it. My heart sank. I knew we would be there for at least the night. There was sand all around, no village, no water, no food. We actually had brought a small jerry can for ourselves but we were going to be seriously thirsty.

We sat up talking as it grew dark. It was December 8th 1993 and there was I under the stars in the desert in the middle of Tanzania and it was no more romantic than the man in the moon! I was completely fed up. I went back into the bus, but someone had brought a load of fish with them on board and the bus smelt appallingly. The person could not throw the fish out as that would attract too many wild animals. Everyone lumbered out the bus and made a circle and huddled together to try and sleep. We looked like a bunch of cowboys on a wagon train!

I felt this appalling pain in my leg, just under my right knee. It was unbearable and I felt I was having a heart attack in my knee. Pauline just told me to be quiet, it was most likely an ant that had bitten me. I felt really deflated and put in my place, but the pain did not subside, if anything it was getting worse, the pounding throb of pain was awful. A few days later Pauline told me that she had seen a scorpion scuttle out from under me in the sand, she told me it was an ant to keep me calm, because she knew there was nothing that she could do stuck out there.

The night passed, I huddled in close to the Italian priest and Pauline huddled close to me. Indeed morning did break and we all looked worse for weather. At 8am the sisters appeared with a tool to take the tyre off and in we all clambered ready for the next leg of our journey. Twenty minutes later, we heard an awful bang AGAIN. Yes, the new tyre had just blown, the bus trip was cancelled and we were all to fend for ourselves the best we could. I was raggedy and itchy and still in pain with my leg, what's more I could have killed for a cup of tea.

After only half an hour a long-based land cruiser came flying along the road. The Italian priest jumped out and was nearly killed trying to stop the car. There were Indian priests in the car who said they could give us a lift two hours down the road and drop us at some village where busses did come through on their way to Arusha. We arrived in this village where we were told the next bus would be 4 o'clock. It was now 10am.

We went into this teahouse and ordered three bottles of cold water and one huge pot of tea. Six bottles of water later and two more pots of tea later we all felt a little healthier. Fr Mario got a room for the afternoon and we all piled in and had a bit of a sleep and went out to a barrel of water in the back and had a bit of a wash. We had our tickets and right enough the bus which could hold about 50 people arrived on time. However, at least 100 people squeezed into the bus, there was no way any one of us was going to wait for the next service to arrive. We all knew that we were going to be late arriving at the border and decided to cross that bridge when it came.

We took off like a scud missile it was unbelievable. The conductor stood on top of the metal bars on the seats to pick up the tickets and money for the journey. He was standing above me for a few minutes and was dripping sweat. We were all on fire and we couldn't open the windows for the dust. The smell of us all was powerful!

Just before dusk the bus came to a screeching halt. No one could see anything bar red cloud dust, but all of a sudden we heard a wonderful clink clink clink. It sounded familiar, but I was wondering if I was seeing a mirage coming towards the bus. I shoved the window open fast and started screaming "three, give me three!" Yes, it was either a candid camera thing or it really was "the real thing!", a young Tanzanian boy running towards us with a full crate of Coke! I flung money out the bus to him and landed a great prize of three Cokes. We guzzled it down without a swallow just in time for the bus to take off again and for us to throw the empties back at the young lad. Good God that could really just have been a Coke a Cola ad'.

We headed for a town called Singida which would mark the half way point of our journey. It was there we were meant to stop for the night as there is a curfew, no transport is allowed to travel at night. However, when we arrived there the bus driver bribed the policeman and we were allowed to continue. There were five of us on the two seated seat. It would be impolite to describe how we contorted our bodies to manage our positions, but most of my body was now numb and that helped the pain in my knee.

Dawn came on the second day and we were still alive. The bus stopped early on and a crowd of people got off. It made it possible for Pauline, Mario and I to sit together. The three of us relaxed and fell asleep in unison and coordination. We were perfect. If one turned to the right, we all turned to the right, if one turned to the left, we all turned to the left.

We arrived at Arusha midday and easily got a very nice bus to take us the five hour journey to Nairobi. Our next hurdle was the border and our visas were one full day late. We were sent in and out of a few offices but I must say they were very kind to us when we explained our predicament. They must have seen we were filthy, smelly and carried an air of desperation about us.

We were through and arrived that night in Nairobi at about 8pm. It was dark and far too dangerous to try and make it into Thika or the slums of Kariobangi where I would be stationed. I knew nowhere in Kenya, so Mario kindly took us to a hostel. The caretakers of the place just looked at us. I was red all over from the dust, I was very smelly and my clothes were a disgrace. I tried to hold my head up, but all I wanted was a shower and fluids, then bed.

That night we all went out for a meal and the next day drove to Thika where the sisters were having a meeting. It was the end of a four day journey we had travelled together. None of us will ever forget it.

Like every African country, it had its beauty and uniqueness. Traditionally, the sisters had run schools and hospitals, but recently had handed over these institutions to African Congregations. We were all now doing such a variety of jobs that were fascinatingly different. I had no job waiting on me. I was to create a job which meant a lot of home work.

There had been awful political and tribal trouble in Kenya that year. There were Kenyan refugees or, as we called them, displaced people. Hundreds of Kenyans had been moved/displaced from their own homelands. There were many missionaries staying and working with these people and the conditions were bleak. Some of our sisters took turns in staying and helping out.

I travelled up one Christmas Eve to bring up supplies and also to wonder if this could be a place where I could work. We went north past Nairobi, and inland. We passed the well-watered and lucrative flower growing nurseries and travelled and travelled. The road was getting worse and the dust and heat thick. We came over a hill and there they were, the displaced ones. It was a terrible sight to see. A vast sea of plastic tents, with hundreds of people. The bus stopped and supplies unloaded.

We met the priest who was staying with the people and some of the nursing nuns. It was an eye opener. The displaced people asked us to come and see their living conditions. The tents were tiny and whole families had to squeeze into them. One lady asked me into the tent and stay there five minutes. I did and could hardly breathe, it was like a furnace during the day and an igloo at night. Their food was meagre. Food in Africa is brought from the fields and gardens; when they become displaced they are removed from the source of their food, leading to starvation. The only thing keeping them alive was the supply brought in by the missions. The government refused to hear anything about it.

That evening the priest just sat outside and started celebrating Christmas Eve mass. There was dust, hunger, poverty everywhere and I felt that I certainly had celebrated the poverty of Christ. The poverty of Christ was all around me in these Kenyan people. I just propped myself up at the back of one of the jeeps and sighed. I remember looking up at the sky, the stars were just becoming visible and I thought of the billions of lives living under the one sky and how utterly different they all were.

We travelled back to our home that night, all a bit muted by being touched by such destitution that day.

Morning in Assisi

Kenya: the "BOYS" getting ready for the football match in Kariobangi, Nairobi. Bernard, far right, and myself, far left

Bernard and myself in Nairobi

Me outside the convent in Kariobangi

Ireland 1984: Bishop Lamont and myself. 1st profession

Ethiopia: the Saturday morning coffee ceremony

Kenya: part of the slum area in Kariobangi

THE KARIOBANGI SLUM

The war broke out in Rwanda and it seemed bad. The house I was living in was one of the many slum areas surrounding the city of Nairobi. There were hundreds of thousands in Kariobangi slum, some estimated over half a million. The advice I got was, get out every day and don't come back till later on. I took on that advice as I had nothing else to do.

How can I describe Kariobangi? Beside us was a huge open sewage vat which was not closed in. If the wind was blowing in the wrong direction then you were blown out of it. We put up bags of charcoal on our veranda to absorb the smell. There was also the Nairobi city dump beside us which was pungent too. That place was like the description of Dante's Hell.

The first day I walked out of our compound right down into the heart of the slum to a very dangerous place called Korococho. There were just people everywhere, walking God knows where. The shanty houses were old corrugated bits of iron put together, some mud houses with iron roofs and others made of steel kimbo tins. The kimbo tins were the margarine tins. When enough of them were empty, they could be battered flat and soldered together to make a house. It was an amazing sight.

I walked down and down the Korococho road till I saw what the sign said was a clinic. There I met a very nice girl who said she was the nurse there. The clinic was a bit lopsided and overlooking the Nairobi dump. In front of this dump was a huge crater filled with water. I was to start my education that day. She showed me the dump, it was a mountain range of muck. All over steam, smoke or poisonous gasses were rising. Huge Malabu vulture-type storks were everywhere and then there were the people. There were adults on one part of the mountain, all picking up metal, paper, tin foil. Anything that they could recycle or sell. Further over were the kids, she said. You don't go near the kids, she said, as they were too dangerous, they would cut your throat in a second. I completely trusted her judgement. At that moment a Nairobi council rubbish truck arrived on the scene. I saw the Vulture make a run for it and then I saw the kids running to the lorry to try and beat the vulture, too. The battle then erupted between birds and children. I was aghast with what I was seeing before me and my eyes hurt. I thought I really was standing before the throne of hell.

The average age of the children was between 10 and 14. They were living and dying on that hill of hell. There were boys and girls and they all survived by being high on glue. When the girls get pregnant, they deliver on the tip and they have not a clue what has gone on. The new born is often dropped into the crater lake. Often, she said, the 10 and 12 year olds are so depressed or so high on glue that they commit suicide by jumping into the crater lake too.

I spent the day with her and with a young man who spent his mornings picking rubbish from the dump. He told me he managed to make enough to eat, but kept away from the children as they were very dangerous. They scavenged out of the rich people's rubbish for bits of food to keep them going. They had all been there for a long time.

My mind was blown and heart ripped out of me. These kids were all orphans. Their parents had died most probably of AIDS and they had to crawl through life literally surviving hour by hour until it all became too much for them. How evil. Children should not have to live this way. A quotation from the Gospel of Matthew kept coming at me, "A voice was heard in Ramah, sobbing and loudly lamenting. It was Rachel weeping for her children, refusing to be comforted because they were no more."

I wanted to roar so the sky would break open and God would come down and relieve these children of their burden. These kids would never know joy, peace, fun and love.

I went back to the clinic a few times to keep educating myself. Once I went with the other boy to the edge of the dump, but he told me to go back as I could get killed. I did as I was told as I did not want to put him in danger.

One day on my daily slum walk I saw some lads hanging round at a corner. They called me over, they were high on drugs. I sat and talked for a while, while they sussed me up. I had absolutely nothing on me they could steal, so they lost interest and I knew I was safe.

Every day I met them and one day they called me over again. We had a great conversation. They were all sitting on a sofa outside in the dust. I sat on the edge. They asked me what I was up to and I told them that I wanted to learn and shared with them so far where I had been and what I had seen. They were all smoking pot and nodding and shaking their heads in a spaced out way. I asked them what they do. One started to laugh and said, "Oh we are the BBC."

"Oh," I said, "What's that?"

"We are the bad boys' club, the BBC!"

I laughed and thought, very smart. They continued telling me what their jobs were. They went into town in a group and would steal from anyone they thought an easy target, they'd work as a group and usually get away with it. They would never steal from anyone in the slums, only people who had a bit. Indeed I realised one of the Italian sisters had done some work with these boys. One day a person she knew had her ring stolen in town. The sister got in touch with the lads and asked could they get the ring back. Indeed they did and proudly presented it to her.

One day I was chatting on the sofa with them and we were in a sea of pot smoke when all of a sudden there was a terrible scattering of them all. I was left alone swiping away the smell of pot when the police came up to me. I smiled innocently, choking on the boys fumes they had left behind and said to the police that I hadn't a clue were they had all gone. Indeed that was the truth and I felt abandoned sitting alone on the sofa. Half an hour later they all came back. The police had gone and I asked what went on. Well it was an obvious small drugs raid at 11 o'clock in the morning. The lads laughed and said that they are the very ones coming into the slums at 5 am to supply them, 11am jail them. My naivety was being shattered every day. It is one thing to know stories, but another to be part of it.

The BBC gang showed me different places around the slums, but said that I should cross the bridge and see the other side. I did one day. I wandered down again on my daily outings and ventured to an area I had never been before. Right enough there was a bridge which looked sturdy enough. I stepped on to it and the next thing a young boy crossed me with his machete: I was to pay! I looked and

95

I had a shilling in my pocket and handed it on, he stepped aside and let me cross, only to have another young lad on the other side cross me with his bow and arrow. I was done for. I emptied my empty pockets out and looked pleadingly at the lad with the machete. He nodded and let the stupid white woman pass.

I found out later that in fact everyone had to pay these two boys' protection money to get across the bridge safely. Well that is one way to earn a living. It was a great short cut through the slums, but I decided not to take my chances there again. I was learning so much about urban living and it was pretty hellish. HIV and AIDS seemed to be the common factor in all the poverty I was seeing. Something had to be done, but what?

I decided to go in another direction this day and kept walking. I saw a few people hanging about this place, they seemed a bit drunk, rough and suspicious. I reckoned I had been passing a number of bars and brothels. I kept walking and stopped at one door. There was a man cooking intestines on a charcoal grill, there was a small sheet partition separating the grill from the latrine which was an open hole in the floor and there was a couple doing their business in the corner. Everything was out in the open, in plain sight for anyone to see. It was also the entrance to the bar where the girls would start the chat up.

I stood there frozen, wondering what the hell was I doing here or what could I do in this brothel. The answer was that I did not know. All I knew was that it was a place that was open. A big Kenyan woman came out of the bar and stood looking at me. She was a big mama, even bigger than me, with her hands on each hip. I thought, "I am in trouble now and the clients may have a free sumu wrestling match to entertain them." She then broke into a huge smile and greeted me and welcomed me into her bar and brothel. Her arm was around my shoulders escorting me past the latrine, which was being used by a drunken man, and the two in the corner having sex. I was sat down and offered a drink.

The room was fairly big and had about eight working tables. The bar had an iron grill and locks galore. It would have been easier to get into Fort Knox than there. The woman sat down and introduced herself as Beatrice, the owner of the establishment. Her father was the barman and was wanting to give me a drink. It was noon. I decided that for this situation I was a person who never touched alcohol, so the dad belted out and five minutes later arrived with an unopened bottle of Fanta. They never let me pay for it.

I kept coming to the brothel, most mornings. There were a good number of clients and usually there were three to four girls in the afternoon. Beatrice never minded me coming to visit as long as I did not interfere with her business. Usually I sat at a table, let the girls do their table chat, then out to the corner to do their business. They usually came over and sat with me for a while till there was another customer. I never pried and they did all the chatting mostly; I just sat there and listened. They were drunk most mornings but still coherent.

Beatrice looked on me as an addition to the family and was very protective of me. One day I was standing chatting to her and suddenly she took this enormous swipe at two of the men. She had heard them whisper if I had any money on me they would get it; well, they never pestered me again, no one messed with Beatrice.

Once, again, the girls told me that they were HIV positive. I had guessed or nearly presumed that, but it was sad to hear. They had the usual story of coming to the big city and getting caught up in their job. There seemed no way out for them.

One day, they invited me over to see their house and have tea. I thanked them and said I would love to. They were a bit drunk that morning, but I followed. In the slums there are just open sewage gullies which you have to jump over or walk around. I usually walked around them, but this morning the two girls jumped over and landed safely on the other side. I who was stone cold sober jumped, missed and landed in the sewer. Well the shrieks of laughter peeled out as I was indelicately pulled by two drunk prostitutes from the ditch smelling not of roses, but that which is very good for the roses' growth! They grabbed me up and dragged me upwards and onwards to their home. We walked through what I called goats alley. It was a very bloody muddy place where they slaughtered goats on the street. I had the feeling they slaughtered more than goats there.

The girls shouted to the men there that I was ok, I was with them. I must have looked a sight covered in shit up to my knees. I arrived at their tiny room. They were very kind and hoofed out the fellow who was in the bed sleeping. We had a cup of tea, then it was time to go back to work. I let them off as they went back to the bar and I went back to the convent.

I always tried to get home by 4 o'clock to get the dinner on for the other two sisters I was living with who actually had jobs. We would pray eat and stay in at night. There was no official curfew in Kenya, but as I learnt later, if you are out after dark, you are fair game. During this time I was also volunteering to work in a place called Maria House. The women there were wonderful. They were social workers and administrators who worked with single women with children. Many of the girls had been raped or were surviving by prostitution.

Some of the babies were known as "Flower babies". I thought, "Is this the 60's again?" I was later told, "No, not flower babies, but *flour* babies!" I still did not know what that meant so as usual they had to spell it out for me. There were women without husbands who were trying to survive by roasting maize or needle work. At times they just had no money, so no food. They prostituted themselves out for some flour to make bread, hence the label, flour baby.

I worked with these girls, giving talks on pre and post natal care, mostly regarding nutrition. I was proud because I gave these lessons in Kiswahili! There was general poverty everywhere. Boys who had been caught as thieves were regularly "necklaced". They say that this ritual came from South Africa, where a tyre was put around a thief's neck and petrol poured into the tyre, the boy was forced to drink some petrol and then set on fire. No one would come to the aid of a thief, especially not the police.

The small street children continually gnawed at my heart. It was pathetic to see them wandering stoned out of their heads with a glue bottle stuck to their noses. Indeed sometimes it looked like their noses were rotting off of them. I was learning so much about life in the slums. There was a common thing coming up all the time and that was HIV and AIDS.

THE STORY-TELLING PROGRAMME

There was a seminar in Uganda on AIDS. It was to be given by a group known as Youth Alive and was established by one of our sisters. I travelled over to Uganda by bus. It was a moving moment, in some ways; going back there was very unreal and seemed like another life time ago. I never travelled up north to Gulu as it was still a very dangerous part of the world.

The programme was started by an MMM sister who developed a process of 'story-telling' taken from Gerard Egan's book 'The Skilled Helper'. It was like the hardware. The software was all the songs, plays, acts and prayer which was developed by our sister and the youth alive team. The combination was electrifying. It was brilliant and helped me personally identify some of my pain inside myself. I knew myself I needed healing. I was holding pain in and I knew one day I was going to explode. The story telling process was in three sections and each of these three sections also had three parts to it. It consisted of, stage 1: Telling the story, focusing on certain aspects of their story and exploring blind spots in their story. We used general questions such as, "How do you know you are popular?" "How do you spend your free time?" "What pressures are put on you and by whom?" and "What is your life like today?" Other questions to focus on specific behaviours are "What happens at discos?" "What happens at times of celebration?" and "Can a girl or boy say No and what will it cost him or her?" Questions used to find the blind spots are, "What really causes Aids?" "Is playing sex the real problem?" "What traditional practices may spread aids?" This is stage one finished and it is important to really explore this whole part of the process. Stage 2 is about looking at alternative goals, exploring what you really would like your life to be like, critiquing this and then looking at the possibility of a new picture for yourself which involves new choices. Stage 3 is about committing yourself to action, so what will I do, how will I do it and then do it. A full programme takes a week and it was powerful.

I came home to Nairobi and decided that this storytelling method was the answer. I had just spent six months wandering around the slums doing nothing else but listen to stories being told. Everyone had a story to tell and everyone deserved to be listened to without judgement.

It was a great process. The programme lasted seven days. There were specific questions, which had been devised throughout the process, to be asked. You went through from superficial to deep stories, sometimes told, sometimes acted out. Art was used; song, mime, everything and anything. All I knew was that it had worked on me and I believed it could work on others. I invited Youth Alive to come over to Kenya. I booked a youth camp and prayed that money would come. I had a good crowd of folk picked, young leaders from all over. I was ready, I had no money and there were six weeks to go.

I knew I wanted to start this programme in Kenya. I needed a team of young capable people and I did not know were to get them. I spoke to the Italian fathers and they told me that if I wanted to be involved with the parish and the street boys, there was a man I should see who worked for the street boys in his own time and sold Mangoes on the street during the day. He was early 20s and I should approach him.

I was told where his stall was and right enough there was a young guy sitting under an umbrella, with his mango stall, scouring the newspaper. I went up to him and said, "Are you Bernard?"

"Who's asking?" was the sour reply.

I introduced myself and told him what the priest had said. I also shared with him about Youth Alive and asked if he would be interested in coming to the programme for the week. He was, but if not working would need help for his family for that week. He was right, he was committed and we forged a brilliant team together.

Ben, as he was known, felt that we could do the process with the boys he was working with down in the slums. He came round to the convent and we devised a plan together. It would mean going out into the slums at night, but I'd be dead safe, he said, "as the lads who may be your attackers will be the lads we will be working with!" That assured me no end, but it was true. The street boys would escort me to and from the convent with Ben and we were both as a safe as houses!

These boys broke my heart. We would go half way down the slums to our meeting house. As yet the priests did not want them in their compound. They had had loads of nasty break-ins, so in fact there was no judgement.

It was very dark and there was just a tilly lamp for light. We had a good number of meetings with them just to talk and listen to their life's story. They were all aged about 15-20. They were big lads. They looked after themselves in their gang, they cared for each other and stole with each other. They survived by sharing their stolen goods with each other. Pot, booze, sex/rape was the name of their game.

We told them after a good few weeks that we were going to a meeting about young people and when we came back would they be up to hearing what we had to say. They said, why not. Ben was the leader of this group, he was my boss. It was a great working relationship where we exchanged leadership roles frequently.

We went to the training programme and it moved Bernard as deeply as it had moved me. I saw a change in him immediately. He wanted to get back and share the programme with others and all the boys. We devised another plan in the convent and carried on with our weekly night ventures into the slums.

Ben led the programmes. The boys said that life equalled pain, so life became about how to relieve that pain, how to survive and how to fend off the inevitable death.

At one of the meetings Joe, one of the lads, came to escort Ben and I down to the meeting room. He was a big lad, over six foot, but as I saw his face that night he looked like he had gone ten rounds with Mohammad Ali. What a mess, his face was brutalized, I hardly recognised him, his face was pink with the skin that had been ripped off him and swollen badly. He couldn't eat, but could only drink. I asked what had happened and he said that he was thieving and the police got him and beat him up. It was all just part of the survival game as far as he was concerned. What struck me deeply was how the other boys rallied round to care for him and over some weeks he healed, while faithfully coming to the meetings.

101

One of the boys just didn't show up one meeting. We heard he had been jailed and died there. Another was killed on the streets. I was over in Uganda when that happened. Bernard told me about the funeral. The priests were not available, so Ben took the service around the grave. All the boys stood around the open grave with booze and weed. They splashed booze on to the coffin like holy water and said their prayer, they smoked weed and flung it in beside him like incense and said prayers and they all waited for Ben to come out with an actual prayer before they covered him up in the protection of the soil. I believe that that was a true funeral. Where was God? I know He was there in them and among them that day.

For sure my mind, soul and spirit were expanding. How I seem to have changed since these early nursing days in Edinburgh. I suppose life changes us all. The "Church" seemed very small to me. It seemed to want to hold just the "worthy" people, but I know that God contains all and that is the difference.

I still kept in touch with Maria House, but one day they contacted me with a request. They had always worked with girls who had been the victims of rape but they realised that the problem was that they were not dealing with the boys who did the raping. They only knew of one person who had a rapist boys club and that was Ben and me. They would like to work with the boys and see if there could be any solutions to some of the problems. They had a couple of trained social workers who would like to work with the boys to see if they could help.

I spoke with Ben. He knew that all the boys had raped for pain relief a lot of the time and felt that Maria House could help them. They were a down to earth group who genuinely wanted to get to the root of the problem in the slums. The boys agreed as long as there were no police and that they would get fed that day.

It was a very good day which led to weekly meetings and sessions with the social workers. The boys needed jobs and an income. Ben and I set up a shoe shining programme and a training programme for wood turning. They were going to be carpenters. Carpenters were some of the wealthiest people in Africa just now as there was an abundance of coffins needed due to the AIDS pandemic. I received money from home and we bought a Lathe. Ben set it up, took lessons himself and with the help of another man started the boys making sugar bowls. I got other equipment and we were eventually allowed into the church grounds again.

The programme was taking off in Kenya. Many groups were asking for the seven day seminar and we were ready as a team to give a very professional programme. It was a great blessing in many ways. It meant that I travelled the length and breadth of Kenya. It was an exciting time sharing the programme at Ngong near Karen, where Karen Blixton had lived. We travelled up the spectacular Rift Valley and saw the wondrous sights of the flamingos on Lake Nakuru and Lake Baringo (which is further afield.) We had seminars up by Lake Victoria and feasted on the delicious Tilapia fish. We saw Thompson Falls and travelled as far as Mombassa for programmes. There was a need for a programme like ours and it was being talked about throughout the country.

I was lucky to have my mum and two sisters come out to visit me in Kenya. Clare was doing some work in Uganda and Kenya, so it was great when we met up there and Mum came to see what I was up to in this delightful part of the world. Frances arrived during her summer holiday break and we were going to make her work! The boys, after the behaviour change workshop, had wanted to play sports. We had acquired sports equipment, Ben had found a field to play football in, so all we needed was someone to referee the match. Frances was coming out on holiday, so who better to get than a football buff like her. She agreed gingerly to the task.

Off we went, just at the bottom part of the slum there was a field of sorts. I must say I had never seen it before but Ben said it was perfect for the task. The "boys" had got themselves into two teams so all we needed was the whistle and away we went. Frances was great, she really was, and the boys were playing reasonably well until the ball started splashing into what looked like to me a big puddles of water. I could see Frances tip-toeing around it and wondered why she was so apprehensive about a little bit of water. At half time I was to find out that it wasn't water she was splashing around in but raw sewage!

The boys were having a ball. It was so good for them and to have an outsider coming to referee them was even better, but poor Frances. She was truly valiant that day and when we finished, we belted up "goat alley" together, had a shower, a chicken in a basket and a Tusker beer in appreciation for what she had done. It was great fun, everyone enjoyed it and no one got sick, thank God. Later in the holiday, Frances and I went off to a lovely resort in Mombassa for a week or so and it was heaven and a change from the slums of Nairobi.

Ben and I continued getting ourselves trained with skills to facilitate the Youth Alive or, as we called it in Kenya, "The Education For Life Programme". Our first attempt at a small group of boys in the parish was disastrous, but we strived on getting more expertise. We asked the Ugandan team to come over again to give another programme. It was brilliant. We managed to get all the "boys" to it.

At the introduction of the week we all had to say who we were and what we did. It was a great time for these lads to say their name and their occupation was carpenter. It was also a reprieve from their daily grind of trying to find food, which was supplied by the live-in course. The food was basic but sufficient. We all stayed in bunk beds and we talked and talked the night away. The boys were great that week and wondered if God could love them. Their lives were more desperate than evil.

Slowly, and one by one, most of the boys died; some kept coming with us to the programmes where I could pay them a wage when they washed up for the group, but slowly they all disappeared.

We became more competent and I was managing to get some funding. We gave courses at Maria House and any other place that was open to us. Story telling is a great medium because it leaves people to make their own minds up and have their own choices.

We needed more members in the team and after about one year we found a perfect young man to compliment Ben. He was quiet, shy and perfect to compliment the gifts of Bernard. We also found a lovely young woman to work with us. We had a smashing team, the only problem was that we were not allowed to work in the Deanery or Diocese of Nairobi. False accusations had gone on about me and even to this day I don't know what they were. The Cardinal asked to see me and shredded me. He told me that he would not sign any document that I needed for funding and that I was not allowed to function without an office. I was to find an office by the end of the week or get out.

I couldn't believe or understand what was going on, but people seemed to be frightened that the power of story telling was unearthing stories that should never be told! That was not my problem; my problem was to find an office. Ben and I had been using my car as our office, but now that would not suffice. It was Monday and I had one week to find an office.

I was phoned on Wednesday and told there had been an appointment made for me for the Friday morning. I knew I was for the chop. I asked my superiors to come with me and speak in my defence of the programme. We all went expecting the worst. I walked in first and the Cardinal shook my hand and said he was sorry and the programme must go on. I was gob smacked, a miracle had just happened. We all sat down and he said that he was giving me authority to go to all the churches in Kenya, he was giving me an office in the Kibera slums and that he was going to hospital that afternoon and I was to come with all my paper work to the hospital and he would sign anything I needed for funding. I just sat there stunned, as did my superiors who were with me. We were alive and we had a big blessing from the boss! It was going to take off.

I believe that two African priests had heard of my dilemma and knew the work I was doing in Kenya. One was a Kenyan priest and one a Ugandan, they went secretly to the Cardinal in my defence as they had also heard of the rumours about stories that should never have to be told. It was my blessing and it was a blessing to have my first office in a place that was poorer than Kariobangi.

The work took off. We were a great team. We made time for study, preparation, team discussion, we availed of libraries and any other source of up to date information. We had team interaction and truth telling moments. We socialized with "chicken in a basket" at the local garage, we prayed and trained. Also the team were paid enough money so they could keep their minds on the job.

Eventually it was not good enough to just give the programme. Others wanted training. With the help of an MMM sister who pinned us down, we devised a training manual and a 'trainer of trainers' programme. I now know that this programme that we devised in Kenya has been all over Africa and some of the team members have travelled even further a field sharing this whole process. It was a proud moment as the midwife/initiator of this programme to realise that even today the life of the programme continues. We worked so hard. I was doing 17 hour days and it was beginning to tell.

I was floored one time with a dose of malaria and typhoid. I wanted to die, I felt so sick. I was dying inside too. I was becoming overwhelmed with pain and after much help in Kenya, I knew that this pain was consuming me. I asked to go and get help.

I could pin-point some reasons for the pain, but not all. Everything seemed overwhelming and over-powering for me; nothing seemed to relieve me and I lived in a constant state of "holding on" to myself and my sanity. If I did not get help soon I knew I would break. I knew that the ordinary concern from the sisters was not enough to pull me through; in fact I am sure that my pain was dragging some of them down. I needed to get away before I broke.

RENEWAL CENTRE, U.S.A.

I went to the Renewal Centre, Attleboro, Massachusetts, USA. It was a great blessing for me and a centre which I felt could hold my pain; intuitively I knew this and immediately let down into deeper issues.

My first four day encounter was with a therapist who went through my life story, detail by detail, and put me through a battery of tests, the most disturbing being the Rorschach test. The other name for this test is the " Ink block" test. It is a test to really find out just what your thinking is like. Psychotic or non psychotic. Ten ink block pictures are shown to you and you are to respond to them. I kept seeing dead men's eyes watching me, it was horrible, but the last few pictures were coloured and reminded me of holidays in Cornwall. At that time I could not think whos' dead eyes kept looking at me, but I knew I was profoundly disturbed by that thought. I was told that I was basically a very healthy person but had some very dark moments and thoughts, luckily I was aware that I was heavy with pain. We talked solidly for four days, and amazingly I never once mentioned my time in Africa or any events of violence that I had witnessed. If asked had there been any traumatic events I said no, as everyone in Africa went through looting, shooting and hijacking. It would be like a doctor asking you for any significant medical history; you would never mention the many times over your life that you had caught colds. It was the same with trauma in Africa, everyone would have multiple stories so there was no big deal. I did not feel I was deliberately suppressing anything.

My next venture would be to wait for the report of this four day assessment and meet the therapists who would accompany me through the next three months. What I always liked about Attleboro was the attitude that the people who came for help were basically healthy but had been wounded. This place was to reclaim that inner peace.

I worked with Claire, a bioenergetic therapist and PhD in psychology; she was my lifeline and her professionalism carried me, she witnessed my rawest pain. Jackie was a massage therapist who was 100% trustworthy with my body when I was most vulnerable. Jim, a Vietnam veteran, Shaman and therapist who gave me back my trust in men. Ed, the art therapist who helped open my eyes through art to the horrors of war and show me a path to healing.

What a combination of gifted people to help me through some of my darkest hours.

From My Diary:

Oct 8th 1997

I saw Claire this morning. She really is something else. She has been trying to get me to breathe deeply, bend my knees, and shout out No No No. Bending my knees makes me feel so vulnerable. She kept asking why? Why couldn't I do that? Eventually I collapsed in the corner and told her to keep away, I did not feel safe, I had to have straight knees to have control. She keeps asking what will happen if I have no control. I have no answer for her; all I do know is that I don't feel safe.

She asked me to think about the times I haven't felt safe in my life. Good question. Claire is excellent.

Oct 9th

Saw Jim today, started talking about why I couldn't scream and started to discover the times I haven't felt safe in my life. Told him about Uganda. My attack, the attacks on the compound. The whole thing of the mass death, the no sound, tunnel vision, etc. He started me talking and thinking. He made me repeat the story of the man being killed, then asked me if I felt anything. Well I didn't really feel anything. He asked me if there is anything that makes me feel. I immediately said, "Yes, Time magazine and their pictures." He said which pictures, and I knew straight away it was the awful pictures in Time magazine of the two soldiers being dragged out of their car in Northern Ireland and stoned and beaten to death.

My head spaced out and I bumped into the door trying to get out of Jim's room. I went to Jackie next, feeling awful, and I just started to cry. I have now been remembering the night all

108

the dismembered bodies were brought off the three army trucks in Gulu and I was triage nurse. What a sight, these poor boys were blown to bits. People kept handing me body parts, there were very few of the boys alive on these trucks; then someone handed me a little hanky, I opened it and it was full of fingers, which fell all the way down me.

Jackie worked with me and massaged my head; it seemed to put my head back together again. God I feel bad.

From my Diary Oct 9th 11pm

Again found it hard to sleep, but when I woke up I felt like some armour had dropped off. I sat up and wrote my paper for the group. There are 21 incidents, mostly from Uganda, that I have been frightened of. God, I can't believe that.

As I was preparing to present to the group my adult story, one of the group came into the room to see how I was getting on. He looked at my long list, I told him that I had a belief that all people are good. He looked at me in amazement and said, "Really, after all that awful trauma? Some people were out to do you no good." This statement has hit me and confused me as though a ton of bricks has fallen on me. I do believe that all people are good, but so many bad, bad things have happened to me.

I am so confused, maybe this nice thought and belief system of mine has protected me from seeing the truth that there are many people out there who are out to deliberately hurt and destroy, in other words: Evil.

Oh, I don't feel well now, I'm going to go out for a walk. The oddest thing I find just now is that I am tripping up on everything, maybe that is because I am not used to having a body or being in contact with my body, I don't want this anymore. Had a dream last night, too, that I went into the dark and had my throat cut. It was a great relief and I just wish the knife had gone deeper. I wonder if I have been living with anxiety of the near death experience in Uganda?

The therapy started in earnest and Jim was amazed that I had managed to get through the four day structured autobiography without mentioning any of the trauma from Uganda. The first few days in Attleboro were extremely painful; yet, it was also like an abscess at long last being lanced open, all this pain and mess was being released in a cradling environment.

I remember walking around the Lasalette shrine thinking to myself that I will not stop this process till I find life again. At that moment I made a commitment to live and live well, to search until I found myself again, because I was dead. I knew I could not stop till I found life. For years I had lived in a protective state of denial, but now my desire to live was stronger than my denial, I was in a very safe place with highly professional people who could hold all of my story, mind, body, soul and spirit. I had been given a chance to resurrect. Little did I know the journey that was needed to find new life.

Throughout the whole process of recovery I would have to strip off layers of beliefs which I had denied about my life, this stripping was so debilitating. At times in my pain, I would have been quite happy to die. Sometimes I hated having the gift of hope because it meant struggling on, and I was beginning to understand some bible quotations even better, like "Unless a grain of wheat shall die it just remains a single grain".

All of this made me feel as though I had really stepped off a cliff and there was no turning back once you opened up. If I did not open up then I would die inside and if I did fully open up then there was no assurances that I would survive it all. I truly felt like humpty dumpty, with the breakdown of my defences and with realisation that evil does exist in the world.

Little did I know that this desire to live would thrust me into an awful place of powerlessness. Denial would keep returning throughout my healing journey as I tried regularly to diminish the losses in my life as a way of *avoiding* grieving. Moving into powerlessness and grieving is horrendous, but completely necessary if you are ever to heal.

Trusting both the therapists in Attleboro and the process they had in place for me was a miracle in itself. People who have been traumatised feel powerless and may have many issues with control and self esteem. A normal reaction to powerlessness would be to gain control; to heal, you need to trust your therapist 100%, as by the very nature of the relationship it is not equal. You are being asked to trust, open up, be vulnerable. The therapist witnesses to the story being told. In reality you are put in a powerless, vulnerable situation so as to eventually regain control of life; reclaiming the whole story of your life. Powerlessness and trust have to go hand in hand.

The body therapy I experienced opened me up to feeling very vulnerable. I believe body therapy is a powerful way of releasing the story. The body holds the story and when we disconnect from the story we disconnect from the body, and therefore the mind is in control.

The mind is a fascinating thing. It can forget, deny, file in the wrong place, diminish all sorts of things, whilst the body does not lie. If you are feeling nervous, then the brain can shame you out of your nervousness, but the body tightens, the muscles in the stomach churn, you have butterflies. If you attend to the signals of the body you will always get a warning signal.

Traumatised people are often disconnected from the body, leaving the mind in control. In bioenergetic therapy, the body is attended to by going through some simple opening exercises. When we reconnect with the body, the mind feels totally out of control and this state is terrifying for a person who has been traumatised.

Complete trust in the therapist is essential.

From my Diary:
Oct 28th
One of the guys in the group told his story today. Well I have been feeling sick since then, a terrible nausea, I feel my gut opening up and hell coming out of it. Went to see Claire and told her how I have been feeling, I actually find all this quite terrifying. Claire said, "OK bend over the bio stool." [This is a stool like a Horse which you stretch over backwards to open up you chest and stomach muscles.]

She asked me to verbalise NO, if I could. I felt fine (which

111

should be a tell tale warning for me now) and shouted, "No NO NO." I then got up and things got quiet in my head. I seemed to be detaching. I felt totally numb, no feeling in my face, my eyes could not see Claire, but I heard her saying, "What's going on?" and I heard my voice say back, " I'm in hell, my head, it's ok if you blow it open, it's ok I don't mind."

She told me to sit down on the mattress on the floor, so I did, then she sat down opposite me then said, "Come here, Jo, and lay your head on my lap." I did; and cried. My body just went into the shakes, it trembled and trembled. All went silent. I did not know were I was or who I was lying against, but whoever it was, they were safe and didn't seem to mind me lying there. Eventually I remembered I was in America and I was in Attleboro and this was my bioenergetic therapist beside me. I sat up and leaned against Claire. God I was so scared.

Luckily I was seeing Jim late in the day. I started to come too. I did not feel right leaving Claire's room, but went to bed to feel safe. I began to remember what happened. For some reason, while I was breathing deeply, it opened up the experience when I was pulled out of a car on the road to Kampala.

There were four of us in the car, we had left Gulu very early in the morning. Unfortunately we had not heard the news that Idi Amin had threatened to make his way back into Uganda via Zaire with his troops, so the Ugandan troops were out on the roads in full force waiting to stop the advancing Idi Amin army.

All of a sudden soldiers appeared in the morning light, rising out of the ditches, shouting, yelling pointing their weapons directly at the car. I was sitting in the back seat and thought I was very close to getting my head shot off if we did not stop the car immediately. We screeched to a halt and I thought I saw a body lying dead on the ground. The next thing I knew was that I was being dragged out of the car by my hair by one of the soldiers. The screaming and shouting of the soldiers was unbearable.

They spread eagled me on the bonnet of the car and I felt the gun at the base of my head. I am not sure what happened, but I remember just lying there thinking, "It's ok, you can blow my head off." Maybe the soldiers pulled the trigger and it didn't go off or maybe they didn't. All I later remember is that I was sitting in the back seat of a moving car in silence, we were all alive. I have no recollection of getting back into the car or what happened to get me there, but we arrived in Kampala safely, went to the convent, got a cup of tea and did our shopping. None of us in that car spoke about the event again.

Jim heard this story, I really didn't think it was such a big deal, it had never bothered me before. Jim said that what had happened in Claire's room was that I had dissociated, I was in terror, but there was a difference this time. Instead of having steel at both the front and back of my head, waiting for execution, I had Claire's lap and hands holding me. I thought that was a very sacred insight.

From my Diary:
OCT 1997
That night, one of the guys on the course began to encourage me to do my "mood painting". The art therapist, Ed, wanted us all to do this. I think I am the only one left who has not gone near the art room. God I am such a coward, I am just dead scared to do it, but I need to.

Later that night.

Did my mood painting. Used black paper, white paint all over, threw red and purple all over, then black all around it. Finished in 20 seconds.

Don't want to look at it again.

Powerlessness and art therapy. Again, this type of therapy locks into the right hand side of the brain. The left side is more controlling and the "mood" paintings Ed wanted us all to do were never to take more than 60 seconds to accomplish. This was scary for a traumatised person because, Lordy, who knew what would end up on that paper; most likely something I did not want to see and something I had buried deep inside my skull, never to be let out again. I had imprisoned many of my memories and I wanted then to stay imprisoned. They were safe there, locked. Now Ed wanted me to free them.

Dear God this was all getting too much for me. The pain in my eyes was fierce when I was doing any art therapy with Ed, it terrified me, but Ed was very patient. He saw my first mood painting and commented that it looked like a stage with the curtains (all in white) closed. All we had to do was to wait for the curtains to be drawn back and the actors of the first scene to appear. What was the story behind these curtains?

I did not want to know and felt powerless at the thought of all that unconscious stuff just sitting there waiting to pour out. I was always scared that my subconscious would overpower me and destroy me. I swung between self preservation and trust in the people who were helping me on my journey. When the mind is not in control the journey can be terrifying, a real walk of trust.

Three weeks into the course I completed my second and third "mood" painting.

From my Diary:

I went to bioenergetics today and did some really good work. I thought of the man being killed outside the hospital gates. Imagine, that is sixteen years ago. At the end of the session I was exhausted, the pain in my head is fierce. Claire asked me why I held my head all the time and I replied "My head is sore and I feel the man's eyes burning into my head, I feel so sorry, awful that I could not save him, I'm so sorry I didn't have the courage to save him; and sometimes my head splits off, the pain in it is so bad."

I left Claire's room feeling awful, I just started to feel so bad, so mental. I felt my head was possessed by the man, I felt his eyes; I felt insane and possessed, I wanted him out of my head. The pressure... if I could rip my head open I would. All night I have been thinking that I am going insane.

I drew two pictures of madness, the pain in my head is so, so bad.

The next day I showed Jim my two pictures. It was amazing

what I saw when I really looked at them .It looked like the soul of the man and my soul locked together; it sounds crazy to the logic mind, but it was a relief to see, as this is exactly what I felt, locked into him.

The other picture was of my head exploding. Jim said that there was such a thing as soul theft in a shamanic sense. It would appear as if I had taken part of his soul into me. I had been so paralysed to do anything for him, but was able to make a home in myself for him. Now it was time to let him go to God.

Jim knew of a Shaman who did good work with traumatised souls. All this sort of thing was completely new to me. I knew of nothing in this area, but it seemed to make sense. If I wanted, I could go to Cape Cod the next Wednesday for a session. I agreed, because I could not go on with this pain in my head much longer.

From my Diary:
I saw Claire again on Monday and went really ballistic. I was screaming at the man to go, please go, get out of my head as I can't stand it any more. My head is really sore and in a very bad way, then I said to Claire, "My heart loves him intensely but my head needs to let him go to God; why can't I let him go to God, Claire?"

She looked at me and said, "Jo, he already is with God, just lie there on the mat and pray to God to take him from you."

I was doing that, crying, praying, and I said out loud, "You can go now, you are safe, I'll let you go."

I couldn't believe what I had just said, I realised, for the first time, how safe he was and I could let go, I didn't have to guard him anymore. All these years I had still been trying to protect him.

I went to bed and tried to sleep.

From my Diary:
WEDNESDAY
Went to Trish, the shaman in Cape Cod. What an experience. Spoke with her for two hours on both the experience of the

killings with the man and what soul release is all about. It makes sense that even by mistake, as it was in my case, that you somehow take hold of a person's soul or energy if you love them. It is like when someone you love dies and you feel part of you has gone with that person, you don't feel whole anymore. In a shamanic sense part of your soul has gone with the person you love, or you can keep part of the person's soul energy with you. All a bit confusing, but I know that there is an energy in me that does need released to God.

Trish asked me if I had any guides to be with me. I always had St Clare of Assisi as a guiding spirit for my life, I asked her to be with me as we prepared to lovingly let this man go home.

It was a very moving experience of meeting the spirit within me that needed release, talking with him and allowing him to go to the light. I felt the energy release and immediately the pressure in my head left me.

Never again have I experienced that same pressure, burning pain in my head, when talking of the man. At this point in my story I had a peace that at least he was safe.

I wrote a poem that night trying to convey my feelings of the release:

The Safe Passage
The Passover from death to life.
The 15 year waiting in the tomb of my body, hidden deeply to protect him from the cruel, violent murder witnessed in terror; with agonizing eyes watching; this was a love totally paralysed.
It's over now, the letting go.
The Light waiting for his spirit to be breathed into the embracing brilliance of safe eternity.
The door is open, the Spirits come and in radiance they Passover into Life.

The Renewal programme continued and the input mornings were powerful. But one morning I was dreading. Jim was doing a morning on Grief. I was not looking forward to this at all.

Jim started with the ocean drum. It was just washing over me, it was an easy sound to take me into meditation. I opened my eyes and there was a picture of the pieta. Jim had lovely music on and read some poetry about Vietnam and the sad losses there. It was beautifully painful.

Jim asked each of us to put up on the board someone who was alive who we were parted from whom we loved. Then we were asked to put on the board two people who had died. We had to stand up and write their names and verbally name them. I could put up my dad and name him, but it was so hard to write up "the man whose name I never knew." I sobbed uncontrollably when saying that, I broke down.

From my Diary:

It is time to grieve. We have all been asked to make like the Vietnam veterans "Wall" a grief wall of our own. Lord this is unbearable, I am being flooded with grief. So many horrendous images of awful poverty, destitution and military corruption from Ethiopia are washing over me. The images of the slums and all the stark evil that goes with that of Kenya are drowning me, my own life sorrows. Dear God, how am I feeling all of this? It is like drowning in hell trying to make my own grief wall.

The House of Hell
There are many rooms in the house of hell.
Some rooms are so grey, filled full of smoke, burning eyes so deep that tears can't fall.
Some rooms full of fire it burns deep into flesh.
Some with nails to pierce already broken feet.
Some with broken glass when stumbling bleeds you dry.
There are many rooms in the house of hell, each one taking life away.
Full of spirit souls searching, crying for their mistakes, the forever echo piercing my pain.
The house of hell, the rooms of torture, is there any way

117

out of this abandonment.

Dear God, how can all this be so painful. I don't want to grieve all this, but I feel as though there is a dam, cracked open and I can't stop the water flowing, but it is the anguish accompanying this, the raw pain. I feel I am burning alive.

From my Diary:
Jan 1998
Somehow I know this initial grieving process must happen. I must go through it. It is beginning to soften me like water on dry clay. Strangely, now I am in my next 10 week course in Attleboro, I am letting Jackie "reach" me. I am for the first time feeling as though someone is touching me. I have for years blocked out love, sometimes with big barriers. It is too painful to let anyone near. I spend too much energy holding myself and not allowing the possibility of life touching me. I have armoured myself against the softness of love, I even feel that the armour is in my pores. To receive love is very painful, I don't know if I have the courage.

How strange it is to fear loving or being loved. One who has been traumatised loses that ability to deeply feel and become intimate and tender. Reclaiming that gentleness is as scary as being taken to another planet. However, it is regaining that capacity to love, trust, be vulnerable and intimately loving which makes us human. When trauma happens, especially deliberate acts of evil such as atrocities, you know that evil has won by the diminished capacity to love and be loved. Reconnecting with the power of love is our call to become fully human, this is our greatest gift.

One day when I came home from an intense therapy session, there was a news report on the anniversary of the death of John Lennon. Something in me tripped. Indeed it was like a trip switch that had been activated. I opened my mouth and started... I ranted and raved about John bloody Lennon. I recounted the day "he nearly got me killed in Uganda." I cursed him, blasted him, shredded him. I went on and on and on about him. I was hyper and felt full of adrenaline. I was buzzed up and blamed John Lennon for my brush with death all those years ago in Uganda. After about two hours I ran out of steam and apologised to the poor sister who had listened to my ranting. She had been very kind with me over my therapeutic journey and laughed, saying she knew I would run out of steam at some point. I went to bed, but was badly disturbed. Over the next few days there was a lot on the radio and TV about John's anniversary. Each time I heard his name I took off into one of my tirades. I didn't want to listen to the radio or see the TV as I was made high by it.

Eventually I went to Jim and started mouthing off at him about John Lennon and that it was his fault that I nearly died that day in Uganda. Jim let me rant away till I stopped and he looked at me for a long time and said, "Jo, I was so sad the day John Lennon was shot and you have to remember that he died that day, you didn't!" Well, it was like a bucket of cold water being thrown over me. It had never dawned on me that he died that day at all. I suddenly felt trapped in time, trapped in my fierce emotional state of fury that I could not get the news report on the BBC because John Lennon had been shot. I felt bewildered and confused. I knew it was 1999, but I was still reacting as though it was 1980. Suddenly I realised that I was alive and he had died that day. I was confused and disorientated, but free of my anger.

Jim worked through so much of that time with me and my feelings towards John Lennon and he said, "Jo, you need to do something, you need to ritualise something, you need to say sorry to John Lennon and let him go. You need to have peace in your life with regards to John…do something." I was able to see how trauma twists your logical thinking. All these years I had blamed him for nearly killing me instead of seeing that it was the villagers and soldiers in Uganda who brought me so close to death that day. I was beginning to see how trauma works, how it manipulates and distorts any rational thinking. I was so grateful for my chance to untwist my life and thought processes. I knew I needed to do something to honour John and allow me, too, to feel sorrow for his death, which up until that point I had never felt.

I spoke with one of the sisters in the house and said that I wanted mass to be said in our convent for the anniversary of the death of John Lennon. She looked at me as though I was mad and wasn't right in the head! She said, "well, put it this way, Jo, why don't we have mass for your friend John whose anniversary is around this time." I thought that fine and we did indeed have a mass for "My friend John" who had died in December 1980. No one else knew it was for John Lennon and indeed I have slowly healed when remembering that awful day, December 8th 1980.

None of the process is complete, healing will never be finished and the cycle of learning to trust, reclaiming our inner power, continues. The story stays the same, but the depth at which you take the healing story does change. Layers need to be peeled off to find the soft resilient nature of our true self to emerge. The stories remembered and told, inevitably plunge us time and again into deeper levels of grief.

As I continued my therapy in America, the armour softening went deeper into me. The grief I continuously felt was realising the price I had paid for living with unhealed trauma. There were so many losses, so many wounds. There was the price to be paid for compassion. What is the price of compassion, what is the price of trauma? For me, it is having to live with my eyes wide open and let go of the guilt of surviving.

From my Diary:
Jim has been doing more grief work with us and again the same story, but different depth to the process. I feel The Man looking at me now with so much love, his eyes are like Christ's on the cross, looking at me with love.

I'm not sure I can handle this.

Today, in the art class, Ed played the music from The Mirror Has Two Faces. Ed asked us all what was the mirror for us. I know, from the many talks I have given about St Clare of Assisi. She speaks of the mirror of eternity. The mirror suspended on the cross. She says, look, gaze, consider, contemplate, study your face in the mirror each day. Look at the borders of the mirror and see the humility of his birth, the middle, study his ministry and the centre, his face, the face of compassion. Study your face in that mirror and see if there is a likeness.

I don't want to open my eyes to see any thing, I hate going into churches now as I see The Man's face, torn and broken, looking down on me, I feel I am being haunted by him. I just can't get away from the shame of being alive. Please don't look at me.

I am feeling very isolated again. I hate this feeling, but I can't bear being connected to these eyes looking at me, I wish they would leave me alone, I wish I felt happy, I wish I felt alive.

It is strange how lonely I feel just now. I have spent all of my life for others and for causes, pushing, driving achieving. However, a lesson I am learning now is that you can't receive love and tenderness by these methods. I am having to relearn everything. I feel like a person learning to walk again. Lord, I feel as though I have compacted fatigue.

The process never seems to stop, it just goes deeper. It seems to be happening again, the man's eyes are staring at me and I still can't bear it. I feel I have to start to look at the question of Good and Evil and what is stopping me from intimacy with myself, God and others. I just feel so ashamed at being alive, I am hurting so much.

From my Diary:
Saw Jim today. God it was awful. Talked to him about the murder in Gulu and just how bad the idea that the soldier really wanted to kill or hurt me was.

Jim looked at me during the session and said, "Jo, I have heard this story a hundred times, so what is new?"

I could feel myself get angry as I began to describe the incident again to him. Again he said, "What's new, Jo? You made the only choice you could make."

I told Jim that I was very angry and if he did not sit down I would hit him.

"Yes," I said, "it was a reasonable choice I made, of course I understand the choice I made, of course it is reasonable. I may as well finish my therapy as this is as far as it seems to be going… a good reasonable choice that every one seems to think is OK for me to have made. I saved my life and just watched him be killed."

Jim started to talk and I said, "sit down or I will kill you."

He sat down and said, "Jo, what is different? Yes, the choice you made was not reasonable because it was Evil."

I replied to him, "When the soldier had hit me and told me to shut up or be killed, the man saw me make the choice to live. Up to that point I thought I could save him, but he *saw* me make the choice to live."

I asked Jim had he ever seen the film Sophie's Choice. He had, and I continued, saying, "Sophie made a perfectly reasonable choice, she had to pick one of her children to live and one to die, it was reasonable and understandable, but bloody well evil.

"Tell me, how did she live with that choice? God help me, someone help me, how do I live with my choice? Sophie's second choice was suicide, now that choice I understand, that is an understandable choice. Do I have a second choice, what is it? Or is it only Sophie's choice I am left with?"

I felt so sick of people telling me that I made the only reasonable choice, but it was not reasonable, it was just evil; I had an evil choice to make. I left Jim and could not look at him, I was just so angry. He told me to phone him; I wouldn't. Sophie's Choice. I hoped I could be understood by someone, God help me.

From my Diary:
I had a dream last night that my dad came to me and talked with me. He asked me if I remembered the time I burnt my leg at school and he put on peroxide to the wound and I fainted.

He said "the pain was awful, but were you frightened?"

I said, "NO."

"Why?" he said and I replied, "Because I always trusted

122

you, even in pain."

"Well," he said, "Jo, trust in God still, as you trusted in me."

Dad left and somehow I know this is very important for me to remember.

From my Diary:
Every time I feel that I am getting to the end of my belief in God some small thing comes along to help me. My earth prayer or humus prayer comes to my aid. How long have I prayed my earth prayer? Nearly six years now. It's the toughest prayer anyone could pray, it leaves you with nothing but the soil you stand on. I am so tired of it, though. How I desire my prayer of stillness to come back, I long for it, but my earth prayer is more beneficial.

This therapy is humus and I know God will's me to complete it and I won't stop until He says, Jo, it is finished. It is hard to understand that for six years He has been the one rebuilding me and reshaping me. The building is my prayer as surely as He said to me in Assisi, "Jo, rebuild your own temple."

How this seems to be misunderstood. I am totally exhausted with pain. He carries me in darkness. How I wish I were able to write. I would write a book for people in trauma and the type of prayer life they lead. It is the prayer of the earth. It is the prayer of the poor, one where everything is stripped away and everyone presumes you are turning away from God. The last six years I have never been closer to God, but I have never been in such darkness, pain, dryness and emptiness.

Anyway, my nightly earth prayer sustains me. One day I'll sleep, earth prayer will go and stillness come back. I need to reflect on Sophie's Choice before I see Claire. I can't help but feel burning shame at watching him die; imagine, I used the same words to Jim today that the soldier used on me. Have I touched my own capacity for evil?

Evil:

    1. If you try to understand it, it keeps you in hell.

2. *If you try to touch it to understand it, it turns you into evil as you access your own capacity for evil.*

So how do I get out of this hell? God's choice on Good Friday. Sophie's choice in the film. My choice in Uganda. God must have been in anguish, does evil bring anguish? How do you live with anguish? I know you can turn bitter or find it all so overpowering that you may kill yourself, but I think I have to look at the one person who knows anguish and that is God, and His choice. His anguish must have been unbearable.

Good Friday is the anguish of God's choice. Why??? So that people like me "in hell" might find one person who understands that pain, giving me a chance to live. Can God's anguish comfort me? I remember the look on Sophie's face when making her choice, it was disbelief first then pure anguish. I feel my soul has been aborted by me due to shame. God help me, I feel I am falling into darkness and the only scripture that is coming to me is, "Jo, Jo, Satan has asked for you, but I have prayed for you that you will be strong and when you have recovered you must strengthen your brothers and sisters."

From My Diary:

WEDNESDAY

Saw Claire today and shared all with her. She spoke to me of "survival Guilt". I couldn't care less about that, I just want this pain to go. Claire got me doing some exercises, but I just felt like ripping in half. She said, "Hold onto me, Jo." I did, but my pain is the most unbearable yet.

Time was up. I pulled a cushion over my head and fell deep into despair. I took a deep breath and said to myself, I'm not going to Jim today, I'm not going home; and I saw darkness inviting me in and I said, yes I am going to the darkness. I stood up to go, put my shoes on and was walking out when I heard a voice say with authority, "Sit down" and I did to my surprise.

Claire continued to write and then said "are you seeing Jim today?" and I replied that I had a 2pm appointment, but there was no point now seeing him and I am not going. What is the *point, I come here for an hour, feel awful, go see someone else and feel worse, then wait for five more days till I feel the pain just getting worse. So no, there is no point anymore.*

I stood up, prowling round the room. Claire could not hear what I was saying to her and I ended up shouting at her like a fool, "There is no point as no one can understand my pain."

Claire shouted back that in her life she too had been in pain with every fibre of her body. I just laughed at her, walked away and said, "No one can understand where I have been."

I really made my decision for darkness, I just couldn't go on. Then I heard Claire shout at me with authority, "I've been in hell and so has Jim, I may not have had guns at my head but I have been there. Hell is hell."

I stopped dead in my tracks, I heard something in her voice as well as her words; I stomped up to her face and just stared at her eyes for a very long time. She held my gaze and she eventually said, "You are looking at me as though I am talking rubbish."

I snapped out of the daze I was in and just said, "No, Claire, I believe you, I believe you've been there."

Suddenly it was like a light penetrated my soul; two rays of pure light giving me, in my hell, a path of light to get out. I felt I was staring into Claire's soul through her eyes, trying to see her truth of hell and despair. I looked for hell and all I saw in her eyes was freedom, woman, control and compassion. She had been there because what I saw was not hell but resurrection and she put her resurrected light into my despair to show me a way out.

I was exhausted and went to see Jim. I sat in silence for the first twenty minutes, I just couldn't talk. Then the whole session with Claire came out. All about the light, hell despair and darkness and all I saw in Claire's eyes was resurrection. I told him that I had nothing left to say and was just exhausted.

Jim said I was to hear more and was to listen. He spoke of the place I was in and it was hell.

"There is a big difference between the crucifixion and hell. Hell is rarely spoken of, but Jesus went there and in there He was transformed. The cross is really quite simple compared to Hell."

Actually, I felt that everything I'd gone through so far was easy compared with that week, I don't think I could go through that again. I could carry crosses again, but go into hell again, no, I don't think I would survive. Crucifixion is a place of pain, everyone's crucifixion is different, but as Claire said, "Hell is hell" and transformation is hell.

Jim spoke of the evil I had witnessed in my life, but I had still remained loving. Jim spoke of the need to do something with his life to be victorious over evil, and asked me to be something as a memorial against evil to prove that evil will not conquer. He asked me if the Ugandan man who died would have something to say to me during the killing and if so what would he say?

Jim helped me through a simple meditation to return to the killing scene and look into His eyes. It was painful to do, but the man looked at me with love and said, "Live, Jo, in remembrance of me."

I, too, now like Francis have found my mandate.

USA Renewal centre. 1ˢᵗ mood painting. The opening scene

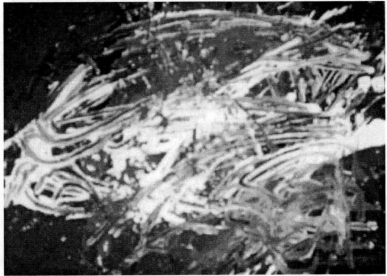

2ⁿᵈ mood painting. The pain in my head

3rd mood painting. Souls connecting in murder

SURVIVAL GUILT

This is a very deep and, I believe, now spiritual problem. The pain of it is nearly unbearable. Many Veterans kill themselves because of it. The word survival guilt nearly seems benign, because it is a very logical label. You can make sense of it, e.g. you survived and you feel guilty. However, it is a very deep wound to the soul and spirit.

I was not sure I was going to survive my healing journey and new worlds were opening up for me. So much of the Church world I felt was infantile, e.g. it is a mortal sin not to go to church on Sunday. When you have battled with the core of good and evil in your life in such an intense way, some of the Church rules seem small, petty and unworthy of the deep riches which are not being accessed.

People are rightly rejecting a lot of the small minded clericalism, which is demoralising and suppressing the gift within. People are crying out for something which is authentic and real. Instead they are often taught to keep rules in childish ways. Where is there room for adults who have walked a path that many clerics have not? Where is the profound message of the gospel being preached?

Much of the mystical presence of God is kept only for the select few who might be "worthy". The childish church will not heal broken souls. Broken souls will discard such silliness with a swipe of their proverbial paw. Broken souls are looking for people, like Claire, to be authentic, grounded and resurrected. Broken souls have no time for anything or anyone else. Broken souls have a certain fearlessness about them. So much has happened to them that they know were they stand with God, there is no doubt in their minds that they are God's beloved and they, unlike Adam and Eve, have nothing to hide.

Little can shake them now. When you have seen a room of hell then there is little in life that can frighten you. Life in general may still not be easy and will always have the same ups and downs as always, but there is a foundation and grounding that you are attached to some thing very good.

It is as simple as that.

When I look at the episode of surviving survival guilt, I see now how terribly wounded my soul was. Little did I know that I was to understand in my own way that my spirit, too, had been shocked by the event.

From my Diary:
It has been 2 weeks since I had my waking dream. I don't know what else to call it, but that I was wide awake, alert, but was it all a dream? I am only recovering now to be able to write it all down in my diary.

A few days after my last session with Claire and Jim, I was at home in the convent and I heard a voice inside me saying, "Jo, this is preparation day, consecrate your life to God, do this in memory of me."

I realised, then, that to remove ourselves from the tree of evil we have to go into anguish and transform the impact of evil and the meaning of evil by living in memorial to the victorious victim. I want to live and witness the victory over evil, because in hell you are unable to share yourself.

Strangely enough during the night I was woken up with a persistent inner voice telling me to get up and read the creed, renounce Satan, and Jackie must witness to this.

I thought this silly, but the voice was very persistent and when I did this and read the creed, I went back to bed and fell sound asleep. Maybe peace at last

From my Diary:
Went to Jackie today and told her. I am so lucky with these guys that they don't throw me out for nonsense. Well, Jackie listened and said that she would massage me and we would be aware of the reconsecration to God.

The massage was really good and at the end, I saw these huge chains fall free, crack and break open. The noise was so loud that I had to ask Jackie did she hear it, too. What are they? I feel a huge weight fall off me. Is this what freedom is?

How do I live in freedom? Or has something died in me?

That night I went home and this is when I had my waking dream. I went to bed, fell asleep, and had a dream. It would be too difficult to explain my waking dream without sounding insane. Indeed the whole thing terrified me, I felt as though my spirit had been snatched from my body and handed over to the devil for ten hours. He played with my spirit. He taunted, tempted and terrified me. He played with scripture and used trickery to catch me out. He showed me a vision of hell to paralyse me.

It was a night of pure spirit. Innocence of spirit was the only survival technique for such a night. Visions opened up to taunt me. All my spirit senses were being hurt. Throughout I clung to one thing and that was God's Mercy. All other things can be debated and twisted by evil, but the Mercy of God is so pure it cannot be touched.

Gospels and scripture can be quoted by the devil and in a devious way, using trickery of words. The evil one cannot twist the Creed. Such bold statements, declaring beliefs, family bonds, intimacy and victory over all things, even death. The devil cannot penetrate the power of the Creed.

In my night of spirit I clung for my very existence to these all powerful truths. I seemed to walk a tight rope of tests that night which battered my spirit. His fury venting at me for the unbinding of my spirit that was occurring. It was then I realised how essential it was that we take the call of deep healing seriously.

I survived that long night, but only just. I felt I had been tested beyond reason. I knew the spirit guides came to my aid that night and guided me safely to the centre of the Trinity. There I felt safe, there I knew I would survive. Within this Trinity I was given three gifts and as they entered my body my spirit came back to me and it was Saturday morning at 10 o'clock.

I was standing with my arms out beside the wardrobe where I had been since the night before. I felt my mind, body, spirit and soul had been electrocuted. I felt I had died and no one in the convent noticed. Whatever this was, I do know that I was too frightened to go to sleep normally for weeks. I do know that when I shared this with the therapists, telling them I was sure I was going insane, they supported me. I do know that from that moment my eyes were opened to the depth of wounding some trauma does, and the depth of healing required. I do know that evil exists and it is bigger than any universe, but the most important thing that exists is love. Evil is terrified of the power of love and evil will never win if we protect that in our lives.

I feel sorry for men and women of evil, they do not know what is in store for them; they are like innocent lambs compared to the evil I experienced in my waking dream. They are just puppy dogs being used, they will have eternal pain if they don't turn away from evil and know the Mercy of God.

I know, too, that there is a difference between soul and spirit. Trauma traumatises mind, body, soul and spirit. We deal with the mind and sometimes the healing of the body, but rarely soul, and never spirit. I believe the devil is delighted with our good works and encourages us, as this does no harm, but, to do the "inner journey" to release our traumatised spirit, well, he is furious and will do everything to prevent us from journeying that way.

Recovery from trauma is long and hard and at this point in my journey I felt as though I had gone through major surgery and was in my first day of recuperation. I was having to learn to be in the world again without the tumour of trauma strangling the life out of me. How could I reinsert myself into my world again? I felt fragile, weak but alive.

I would have to, over the next few months, learn what things would trigger me. I spent the rest of the summer doing mission appeals around America. I felt like a stroke victim learning to walk, talk and live in the world again, everything seemed new and triggers were everywhere, but I was getting stronger and determined to reconnect with the world.

In many respects the next years to come were the hardest and longest yet.

JOHN OF THE CROSS

I was flying home from a weekend of appeal work; someone had put in my bag a book on John of the Cross. I had never read his spirituality before, but as I flicked through the pages I saw some of the headings in the book.

"The soul as a battlefield," it said, "St John's description of the conflict that can tear us apart is as vivid and symbolic as the battle plan of a great general. On the one side are God's own messengers, the good angels, who mediate divine communication to our human form. On the other side is the devil who detects this action and hisses in fury."

"The battle is allowed because it prevents us from remaining naïve about the reality of evil in this world."

These two quotations made sense to me on my journey. I had been feeling for sometime that the soul's encounter with Hades was a preparation for the soul's encounter with God. This encounter strengthens us. God has walked His journey with us, but desires a fuller encounter.

I believe entering these trauma wounds is a prerequisite for receiving the Pentecost call. Resurrection is fragile and the soul needs time to heal, if it is to be strong enough to receive the new call.

Trauma recovery makes you grow up. It shatters every vestige of naivety. Shattered childish images need to be let go and grieved for. There is a terrible emptiness waiting on someone who has survived so far and the adjustment to a world that hasn't seen Hades can be severe. There can be a loss of direction, and misunderstandings become abundant.

It is very difficult to reinsert yourself back into the same slot in life because you have a whole future ahead of you waiting to be rebuilt, incorporating the lessons of recovery learnt so far.

My process continued, but with a new sense of rebuilding. Part of healing is lancing the wound, exploring it and washing it out. Once this is done thoroughly there is the long path to healing by developing a new blood flow to encourage healthy tissue and skin to develop.

This is a long process needing constant supervision to prevent the wound from becoming infected. A lot of vigilance and discipline is needed not to become blasé.

There is an emptiness and an identity cleansing. For so long the wound has been carried, but who are we now when we do not carry the wound but only the scar? There is an emptiness to paradoxically become full. Fullness now means reconnection with self, others and God.

The questions now asked are, "Who am I now?"; "What do I want to do?"; "How do I want to live?"

There is trial and error all along this path. Learning happens every day. As the person rebuilds and connects with life then triggers come in abundance. Triggers feel as though you are going backwards on the journey. Understanding triggers and the adrenaline rush they produce are key to having the courage to move forward.

Emptiness and loneliness harass the person. Life could be easier if "I remained isolated." In that isolation you don't have to deal with triggers and you are in control of your walled-in life. Part of healing is learning to trust others and the world again.

Some people pick up the same pattern of living as before the healing journey began. Occasionally this works, but many find that by repeating the same patterns which originally traumatised you, is not possible to do again. Life has changed, not ended, and you find new limits and boundaries that you need, to keep grounded and vital. Being grounded in the present moment is essential, being aware of your body and the signals it truthfully gives you is your safety net. Rebuilding now has a foundation on reality. Living within the body's natural rhythms, leaving go "causes" and the need to have "intensity": intense moments, intense relationships and intense prayer is key.

There can be a terrible misunderstanding at this point on the journey which can bring profound suffering. Those who thought you had nothing better to do than get "back in the saddle" and continue to intensely journey the hero's way, may feel betrayed by you.

When I left America, I went back to Africa. I had with me my daily plan to keep me alert to myself and safe. I had been asked to share with many communities about trauma and Franciscan studies.

It was a chance for me to get "back" without the responsibility of project management.

In the few months I spent there, it became clear to me that I could not survive in Africa again without seriously compromising my hard fought for new life.I had often reflected on a story which was mirroring what I was going through. I called it the "Sugar Factory Story". This is how it goes,

"I live in a kind community, we call it the sugar factory. While I was living there, I became fragile and sick. I knew I needed help and my community sent me with their blessings to go and get help for my sickness. I left the sugar factory and went to a wonderful place were they diagnosed me with diabetes. I learnt so much about the condition and became so well that the hospital would discharge me. I was delighted and I looked forward to returning to the community. I was gripped with fear when I realized the only food I would get within the community would be sugar. I knew now that if that was the only food that was available to eat I would become very ill indeed. I shared my concerns with the community and asked them if it would be possible to change as a community and bring in a more balanced diet which would benefit us all. They looked at me with sadness and said, 'it is you, not we who have the problem.'

Sadly I saw the story of the "sugar factory" come to life. I had healthily changed the diet of how to live my life and could never again function in such an unhealthy atmosphere.

I needed connection with others who were grounded in their bodies, had boundaries and limits and were willing to be able at times to care for themselves. I needed community and commonality in that grouping.

IRELAND - HARD CHOICES

I came home to Ireland and continued my therapeutic journey, first with Ann McCourt and then with Dr Maud McKee, whom I have now extensively journeyed with for the past eight years. She has professionally and patiently walked with me as I have stumbled through my long rebuilding process. There have been intense moments throughout, but brick by brick I have reclaimed the life God was calling me to.

With undeniable grief, I left Africa for good, and with certainty and terrible sadness left the congregation I had been with for the past nineteen years.

I felt even more lost and empty. My identity as a missionary and hard worker was irrelevant in this new world. This terrible emptiness caused me profound suffering as I tottered around in my new existence. I did not know how to be in this new world, I did not know how to connect with it.

Maud guided me through so many basics that I did not know or had forgotten, from as simple as how to use the "Hole in the wall" to learning to trust new sensations of joy in my body.

At times reconnecting with life could be overpowering and over stimulating. Much of the first few years with Maud was about controlling my adrenaline in situations. Luckily throughout this time I had full time employment in Dublin as a staff nurse, where I gained many friends and reclaimed the capacity to laugh heartily.

It was within the first week of finding employment in Dublin's Mater Hospital that I made a reconnection with a very old friend. I remember meeting Aisling, a young care attendant at the time, who asked me what had I been doing with my life. In reply to this I said that I had worked for years in Africa as a nurse.

"Oh," she said, "So did my auntie Kathleen work in Africa, I think Kenya, but that was a long, long time ago."

I looked at young Aisling's name badge and said to her, "Horan is your last name? Is your auntie Kathleen, Catherine Horan from Mountmellick who worked in Kenya in1980?"

"Oh yes," she said, "That's auntie Kathleen!" I looked at Aisling, asked her her age and what her father and mother's names were. She told me, as I stood in awed disbelief that not only was "Auntie Kathleen" the Catherine Horan I knew in London, but Aisling was the unborn child of her brother's, whom Kathleen had been worried about on our flight out to Africa. How unbelievably strange.

It was over a year before Catherine and I met up. During that time, my friend Robin and I, (who left the convent the same time as me, but for different reasons), grew very supportive of each other. Robin had bought a house, I was busy house hunting.

This was a very difficult time. I kept working with Maud throughout, lots of necessary connections were being made giving me a foundation to live from. It was an extraordinarily hard time. When my life was being opened up in America, there were so many intense moments and cleansings. Now there was intensity but in very ordinary ways. I realise now how much pain there was in learning to live a very ordinary life, e.g. working and house hunting.

It was extremely hard to be ordinary as I had been used to dangerous places and projects, and a lot of the time now I felt lost. A saying I learnt from Jim was "Fake it till you make it". I faked conversations for a long time. I knew how to talk on Africa, project management, spirituality and trauma. I had no idea how to chit chat or find anything vaguely fulfilling in talking about shopping, the latest trends, pop music or children. I often fell silent, with occasional statement contributions to conversations. My connection with Maud was lifesaving.

I felt that most of my life I was acting and I could be real and accepted with Maud. Therapy moments gave me a reprieve from the act of my life. I continued to learn many new triggers and control my adrenaline while still engaging the world. I continued to learn ordinary workplace relatedness, I learnt a lot from some very young colleagues about inclusiveness, ward nights out and simple laughter. I learned to be involved, but had the capacity to let go and move on. I forged new friendships and encouraged myself to go out to places of interest such as the drumming group, the theatre, the gym and the REAP programme for Irish missionaries and development workers.

Life at this time was all about learning. Remaining grounded and living with boundaries and limits will never change. These three ingredients are my rock foundation.

During that period of time I grieved a lot for the nineteen years of my life lost. I believe I tried to do a lot of good in Africa, but the cost had been high. Most people my age had promotion, houses, children, pensions, cars and a circle of friends. I had none of that, but I did have the potential to recreate some of my life.

The previous year, I had completed my Reiki Master Teacher's certificate and I started to use this more effectively in my life. Reiki was becoming a hand of healing for myself and reaching out to others.

I had been interested in doing a counselling course. I had completed my debriefing course and enjoyed it, I wondered if counselling was for me. I went for an interview; some questions asked in the interview were ridiculously too invasive. After all my experience in boundaries, I most certainly felt this panel's interviewing skills were boundary breaking. Some questions asked were more pertinent for a private therapy session rather than for revelation to a panel of people whom I may never see again. I told them this and needless to say I wasn't accepted on that course, so I left the idea of further training till another day.

I had some hard knocks to take when my house deal fell through and I felt a little shattered by it. My family in Scotland were my rocks, but I knew I had to stand on my own two feet. I bought a car, it was a silver Fiat Punto which I was very proud of. Again, Maud was there, sharing my achievements as well as my downfalls; she was my touchstone and I still needed her.

Before I had borrowed my friend Robin's car, but now I had wheels of my own and it was time to meet up with Kathleen Horan Doyle. Aisling's mother had kindly invited me to their home to reunite me with Kathleen. I had learnt that she had come home from Kenya after her year to look after her sick parents. Kathleen was married and had three children. I looked forward to the reunion.

As we had connected so easily and well in London all those years ago, so too we seemed to connect smoothly when we met up. Her children were lovely and her husband a shy big man with a humorous smile. After an hour or so we clicked back into the comfort zone of friendship we had in London.

Before the evening was out, she asked me if I would come to her eldest son Barry's conformation. I was delighted, it was lovely to be involved in family life. If all the therapy was to count for anything, it was for reconnecting and it was happening to me.

Continually I went to Maud. My life was opening up to the feelings of inner joy and happiness. At times I would say, "I need to be here because I am happy." These deep positive feelings were alien in my body and it was frightening to experience them without being overwhelmed and lose my grounding. Every step I took had to be small and grounded. Too much of anything could be enough to trigger an adrenaline rush and I hated these intense moments Conscious living and conscious contact with self and others was the order of my life and the only way for me to be. Too much spontaneity felt too dangerous and it was a minefield I was not ready to cross.

What I did learn was that life was for living and could not be put on hold. It did not matter what you were doing, but if it was done in kindness then I did not have to live with "causes" and "intensity". My continual battle was not to have to live to find a cause. I felt blind so often, but continued making friendships at work and holding onto my long-term friend Robin. We were lucky to have each other as we naturally debriefed and story told the journey of our life together. It was great and necessary to have someone who understood the African connection.

Luckily all my family had visited me in Africa and my sister Clare had also worked there. I was fortunate to have people to whom I could talk and relate to from my experience abroad. I worked with Sr Rita Kelly in the Irish Missionary Union and soon we developed with Fr Paul a workshop for missionaries and development workers. It involved mainly awareness topics of trauma in missionary life. This gave me great energy as I felt I was contributing to the healing of not only myself but others.

We run these workshops every year for missionaries and development workers. Much more in this area needs to be done, but the Church has to wake up to its obvious call.

I went to Mountmelick to see Kathleen and Sean's son, Barry, make his confirmation. It was there I met for the first time Matthew Doyle, Barry's sponsor and Sean's cousin. He surprised me, that is all I can say about him. I was deeply overcome by genuine laughter the first day I met him. I was surprised at my capacity to laugh and felt immediately comfortable with him, and with Kathleen's family, and it was lovely being part of their celebration.

I do believe that Kathleen "matchmaker" Doyle had something up her sleeve, but at that point neither Matt or myself were thinking about relationship. Certainly the idea had never entered my head, I would no doubt need a brick to fall on me or a miraculous intervention for me to open my eyes to the possibility of a relationship with a man.

My life continued, there were awful moments of disappointment on the journey and I had to learn, with Maud's help, how to cope. I felt like Humpty Dumpty who had been put back together again, but lived in constant fear of falling back down my black hole. I did in fact "fall" with regular credit to myself!

Outside influences of deliberate evil, like 9/11, took me by surprise. The constant replaying of the violent scenes ungrounded me. I survived by doing my bioenergetic exercises and listening to Chopin. I learned that world evil still exists, but watching it being replayed was not good for my mental health. Anything that is overpowering in world news, I watch and take it in once; I ground myself, inform myself and move on. I do not nor can I afford to indulge in the constant replaying of the event.

Kildare, Ireland: wedding day, 7th May 2004. Matthew & me, Kathleen, Clare and Frances

The Doyles: Sean, Grainne, Rory, Barry & Kathleen

Matt and myself at Punchestown races

Working on the tractor around the yard

MATTHEW

I was lonely now in Ireland. I was now standing on my own two feet. I knew that life was about making healthy connections and I was able to do that. I may have been fragile at times, but felt it was the right time to move home to Elgin, Scotland, where my sister, Frances, and mother lived. It was December 2002 and I planned to be back in Scotland by June2003.

I had been doing night duty and never minded working Christmas or New Year. I had been working Christmas week and a nurse who needed to repay a night shift asked if I minded if I took a night off for her to repay her owed shift. It was a strange request which meant I would work four nights on, one off, then two on. It was a request which changed the course of my life.

Kathleen phoned me, wondering if I could come to a family work party her sister was having on Friday night, December 27th 2002! I was free, so I could go.

That night was the beginning of new life for me. Matthew, Sean's cousin, was there. Very little needs to be said now. It had been seven months since we first met and at this party we both looked, liked, laughed and easily enjoyed each other's company. I felt "at home" with this happy man and was totally disorientated by this.

I completed my two night shifts and went home to Edinburgh to spend the New Year with my sister, Clare. I shut down the fun I had had with Matt as I had never thought of the possibility of a real relationship and was sure he would not contact me again.

I was back in Ireland about a week when the shy phone call came. It was Matt and he asked, "would it be nice to meet up again?"

I was in a fluster. I knew so much that I wanted to see him again. Wow, I was going to have some story to tell Maud next session!

Matthew is a farmer and is in love with the land. It is his passion. On our first date we climbed to the top of Knockaulin, which is a Celtic historical site in Kilcullen. The view was beautiful on that cold crisp January afternoon, both of us were at complete ease with each other and after three months we knew we were in love.

One morning, I woke up in my flat, I had a picture of Matt in my mind. I realised that his face and smile had totally replaced the constant vision I lived with of the Uganda man's face. I now had a face of love in my soul and I no longer felt defined by my wounds. The power of love is magnificent.

Luckily Maud McKee is not only doctor and therapist, but a married woman whom I felt at ease to share my relationship with Matthew with. Like anyone in a new loving relationship you have to learn and remain open to the voyage of discovery especially now as a couple embracing the world. I also knew that complete honesty about my life was needed. Matthew himself reciprocated honesty about his life. I also knew that he would need to understand more about trauma recovery and its implications if we were to move deeper into relationship.

I asked if it would be OK if we met for a session together with Maud, for him to understand about triggers and necessary living. I now had to learn to embrace my trigger moments as a couple and not as an individual. Matt was open to learning what I needed and I had to learn to ask for help. It was a vital support to me that Matt was willing to learn, it was necessary for our relationship to develop.

My own mother had read a lot about trauma when I had been in the acute stage of recovery and it is so supportive to have loved ones informed. PTSD is a disorder you live with and can live well with if you have the correct support system. I find it mind boggling to see all these self help books showing you a wilful way to recovery and quick fixes to get you back on your feet, repeating the same old patterns in your life, maybe a new job, but same pattern. There is no quick fix to most difficulties, only new ways to live with them.

There is something beautiful about journeying a journey of transformation. You can become surprised by the new creation and have a new capacity to be filled with joy. My relationship with Matt was doing just that.

Both families seemed happy that we had met one another and seven months later we were engaged to be married the following May.

We took life one step at a time. The greatest ability we have is our truth and capacity for love and forgiveness. I have reconnected with life in a deeper way than I could have imagined. I live well, continually discovering new triggers. I need to be regular and grounded, I need to sleep well and be able to take surprises which give rise to spontaneity and creativity. I need to protect myself if the atmosphere is too chaotic, scattered or disorganised.

One of my insights now is how we misuse time and how proper use of time is a great healer. If we reconnect to time with respect, I believe we can change. If we learn to move at an organic pace there would be no need for grabbing at time to create space for ourselves. Today's society is so inorganic. It is manic and spinning, there is little time to live organically. Fast communication has never created more space for ourselves or established deeper intimate roots with self or others. It has sped up life and removed us from its very rhythmic nature. It has compartmentalized time till we feel we are now masters of it. All this speed gives us less time, brings on strain and stress, bringing us to ungrounding, adrenaline rush and burnout.

Recovery allows time to have time to have its natural ebb and flow. Time's ebb and flow naturally detoxifies our spirit and body. It is very obvious in the medical profession that once in a spin it is painful and difficult to slow down, take time out. I have learnt much from the natural rhythm of plants and flowers. Planted in the right soil a plant thrives to become only what it is called to be. It grows and with that energetic burst blooms for a limited period of time before wilting and dying, then, lying, regenerating in the earth till next year. When recovered, it blooms into beauty again.

Watching the seasons is a true healer. How we force fruits out of life at dormant times, how they seem to be fed abnormal encouragement to fruit where they should not fruit and in the wrong season. Lack of ability to wait on God's time to usher you into fruitfulness gives birth to weak and tasteless fruit.

Recovering health means allowing nature's flow to move through you. How we need to fill ourselves with purpose, goals, vision and aims. Just to sit with a sense of nothingness is to miss magnificent activity.

The healing journey will last forever, but my journey has taken me away from intensity to find ordinariness and peace. It has brought me a new found happiness with Matthew my husband. We have learned the joys of working together. I have given up my job in nursing to work full time in the house, on the farm and in my own healing activities.

Matthew and I have both completed a course in horse management and polytunnel management. We have renovated the farm, stud fencing two more fields, building two new foaling units and stables. We hope that it will be a successful livery yard.

I have also developed my Reiki. I have a cabin built which is multipurpose. It is a lovely quiet place to just sit and also to have Reiki done. Matt and I built a healing Labyrinth in the yard, too. It is made from cobblestones and is quite beautiful. It reflects all our journeys of life, walking in and through darkness to take time in the centre to regenerate and allow ourselves to make new choices for the remainder of our journey. It is a wonderfully reflective path being able to remember people we have met, loved and forgiven, people who have helped us to grow in our lives and incidents which although pain filled have given a new vision. Many people have come to walk this healing path, which has been used for this purpose for centuries. The labyrinth that we have created together symbolizes all of our spiritual journeys.

Matthew has brought me back to finding simplicity in my faith. Each year we bless the fields and journey with people when they walk the pilgrim way. My life is content as I move deeper into the mystery of what living is all about.

At home in Kilcullen, a neighbour walking the Labyrinth that Matt and I created

My mother and Matt, blessing the fields at Easter

A SUMMARY OF THE 7 STEPS TO RECOVERY

THE SPIRITUALITY OF TRAUMA

Over the past 10 years I have often reflected on my journey of trauma recovery and have asked myself, "Why do I continue and has it been worth it ?"

I believe it has been a tremendous spiritual journey. I ponder on the people I have met and my therapeutic relationships, reflecting for me the image of a patient compassionate God. I know that it has been a passage of my souls' journey to God.

Trauma is any experience that overwhelms your normal coping mechanism, leaving you psychologically and spiritually wounded. There are a range of trauma's and traumatic events which many experience, varying from serious accidents to natural disasters, to violence perpetrated on people by another.

In Judith Hermans book "Trauma and Recovery" she says that when destruction happens due to natural forces such as Earth quakes, tsunamis' and tornados she would call them disasters, in comparison, when disasters happen due to deliberate human evil it would be called an atrocity.

Trauma is overwhelming but only atrocities are in and of themselves evil. It is what the person does with trauma which liberates or destroys. Trauma has taken me on a faith journey and has brought me into a deeper intimacy with myself, others and God. I believe that it is a deeply spiritual yet deeply human experience. It strips away all your known ways of being and throws you into a dark night. There is nothing "religious" about this journey as it moves you "out" like both Francis and Clare of Assisi who left the centre of town to live on the edge were they learnt all their lessons. In fact they should have never been called Francis and Clare of Assisi because they left Assisi, to living on the fringes with the outcasts.

Living and journeying through the post traumatic stress disorder takes you from the centre to the edge, from the included to the excluded from the head to the heart to find in that place, the souls own reflection of God.

By living on the fringe you discover new sight, God walks among us there. Trauma recovery will bring you into rejection, misunderstanding and judgment. It takes great courage to search for the Beloved on the edge. It is a journey of finding ones truest self which lies on the same coin as the Beloved who whispers, "How beautiful you are my Beloved." (Song of Songs)

This journey into the wound is terrifying and it is not for the faint hearted but so often there is not a choice because, "life wounds". The wound that holds terror can hold the blessing. How important it is to journey this way.

I found that before coming into my trauma therapy, I thought I was healthy functional and relational. I did not realize how sick and anemic my Spirit had become. I had "armored" myself against life. This kept me away from my soul, spirit and essence, the very way of being known.

In Trauma therapy, many of my defenses cracked. From within that crack, I began to find "Jo" the woman God always intended me to be. The Joy of healing has been reclaiming this essence within me and learning to relate to others through it. Relationships do flow with greater ease. There is an inner Wisdom, the inner Sophia, who is listened to. Because I see myself, I am less fearful to be known by others, relationships are more intimate and less superficial. As the eyes of my soul slowly heal, my "routine "prayer life with God becomes a " relationship". I now believe the words written in the Song of Songs, "You are wholly beautiful my love, without blemish."

I once heard, "When you have been touched by God you are never the same." and I also know that, "When you have been touched by trauma you are never the same." Is the touch of God the same as the touch of trauma? Trauma devastates and destroys, God renews and rebuilds. Someone who has been demolished by trauma has the unique opportunity to allow the hand of God to refashion the "Living Temple by building with Living Stones." God's touch can, if we allow it, be contradictory. My journey has been painful, but also beautiful. It has been a journey into darkness and isolation which led me into the intimacy of being "Known". When you are known at a deeper level, you feel that you "know" at a deeper level some of the mystery of life which remains nameless. "I call you friends because I have made myself known to you." (Jn 15).

Shame, the first emotion of the Bible, brought with it feelings of "being bad". This is the beginning of the journey into isolation and alienation. The healing road for shame is to "Reveal my all to another". Very often the person may be a therapist, but this is the first stepping stone to freedom. It is a call to BE authentic. It is a call to be "known". In going through Post Traumatic Stress Disorder Therapy (PTSD) therapy, I have come to know myself better and to know the God within me better.

The process of unmasking my hidden trauma has removed me from the trappings that I have allowed to hide the real me. Standing naked and unashamed before God and myself, I have come to really know in my being that I am, "The Beloved of God." I have learnt that the way of healing and reconciliation is to travel into the darkness of my own woundedness. It has been a journey into nothingness, pregnant with fullness. It is a journey with Christ to the Garden of Gethsemane, into the Hell of the Damned and the Resurrection of Easter. It is not yet complete.

In this journey, I have heard a call to live and not just to survive for the first time. A call to compassion and companionship with others on the journey. PTSD therapy has been a journey which has shown me the truth of scripture which says, "My power is in weakness." When you have been traumatized, you literally "Lose your breath" and "Your Spirit." The Spirit is known as "Ruha", the breath of life, the gift of Christ at His Resurrection. The Spirit brings Wisdom, power, Life. When someone is traumatized, the breath and the Spirit are cut off. Recovery from trauma is also about recovery of the wounded Spirit within us. Therapy has helped me reclaim my breath and once again breathe with the Spirit of God.

Trauma gives one the opportunity to see the mystery of life. In my experience, resurrection and reality is only seen in darkness. I have walked the valley of denial, powerlessness, lack of trust, terror, shame, pain, grief and isolation. The gift received in darkness has been accepting my vulnerability, my limitations and finding the wonders of my humanity. By accepting my humanity, I am discovering that life is about "rising" from darkness.

Moving into the 21st Century, we have to look at a new call, a new mission to address the reality of the evil of violence and trauma. People are numb with violence. People are in pain with violence. There is so much evil done in violence, it is impossible to comprehend. We try and address it, but first, we are called to embrace the martyrdom of our own transformation out of trauma. Then, and only then, will our eyes be open to the depths of pain, brokenness and spiritual death that trauma binds us in.

The release of "THE SPIRIT" will come in power, when we choose as individuals to unbind the brokenness of our own lives. In the breaking of the Bread of our own lives, multitudes can be fed with the richness of a body, blessed and broken. There is a new "Mission Territory" and that is the inward journey. We are continually being faced with trauma and we can continue to choose to minimize our collective woundedness, thus missing a life's opportunity to release our Spirit and find the God of darkness. It is there we are asked to accept the "wedding" invitation, to go to the "Passover meal."

The call of today is to transform our pain instead of ignoring it. Trauma wounds both Soul and Spirit. It is like a plant that has been violently uprooted. The wound left in our Soul, and Mother Earth bleeds out safety, acceptance, love, and affirmation. The wound like mother earth remains open, waiting to embrace us as we accept the call to enter into the tomb time, the time of transformation. It is there that "new Birth" will happen. Christian groups have discussed the idea about "New Shoots". Usually this image is of a brand new shoot, springing up from the ground or from the side of a very old tree. New shoots, will spring up from the trauma wound.

The Earth will transform us. "Unless a grain of wheat will die and fall upon the ground, it remains but a single grain." This is a calling to live, not just to survive. It is a collective call to enter the "Good Friday" place. The place of nakedness, of being seen, the place of complete vulnerability and a place of pain. In the face of trauma, Good Friday is not just one day, it is a place of being. The territory is not mapped out, the roads are not clear, but the invitation is for all of us.

Shame is brought about with trauma. It alienates us from ourselves, others, God and the world. The new Adam is "The Christ" who came to bring us out of our shame back into intimacy. Embracing this is a dark journey into faith, believing in the transformation from naivety to wisdom. It is a frightening journey. Christ in the garden of Gethsemane was in terror, till he sweated blood. Part of His terror was seeing the reality of His future. In His terror he asked a friend to stay with him, but they did not understand and they fell asleep. "The way of the trauma wound" is like that. You are misunderstood and often lonely. The call is to remain in the "dark time."

Robert Grant says, "To whom much trauma is given, much is possible." (3.)

I believe this statement, as one to whom an abundance of trauma has been given. I have had many choices to make in walking this journey. As missionaries our lives are about "Contact". As one who has been traumatized, I thought I was very good at "Contact". I worked very hard, had successful ministries and in driving myself more and more felt I was making an impact in the Church. I could not sustain the level of drive that I had. As I chose to move out of "active" ministry to "Walk the Trauma wound" I realized just how fractured and alienated I was from myself. I realized that "doing good works" is very necessary, but many NGO groups are doing the same. Our call has to be different. It has to come from a contemplative stance.

If we look at the violence and trauma in the world today, how do we address this? From a contemplative view? Contemplation is about contact. Conscious contact with self, others and God. Often we are unconscious to ourselves and to the people we live with, but strive and work hard for the people we are called to serve. The gift of trauma is about contacting God through our pain, weakness and vulnerability, thus making our contact with others life giving, authentic and Spirit filled.

RESPONSE TO TRAUMA.

How has the Church responded to trauma? I see trauma in the world like an iceberg. We have responded to the visible signs of trauma, but this is only the tip of the iceberg of the damage of trauma. Our response to war and violence has been by housing, medical, development, agriculture, water and social work. People need these basics for life .Moving down the tip of the iceberg are the justice and peace groups, fighting unjust systems in the world. The call to respond to the roots of the damage done by trauma is a call to go below the water of the iceberg or below the waters of our consciousness. There you will see the HUGE MASS of frozen life, or, our frozen traumatized body.

THE JOURNEY THROUGH HEALING.

The journey through healing is to reclaim the frozen body.I reflected on the journey I made through my time in America and again on my on going journey with Maud in Dublin and came up with seven steps needed to embrace the healing journey, they are:

Step 1. Denial.

The first step on the road to recovery is to look at DENIAL. The desire to really live has to be stronger than the unconscious desire to just survive. This is a small sentence but if it is not fully embraced, then the healing journey is a theorized journey, rather than a lived one.

Step 2. Powerlessness.

The body needs to be "thawed", so blood can flow through the system again. When someone has been traumatized they have been put in a position of severe powerlessness. In powerlessness, a person's sense of self has been injured. Missionaries who have witnessed horrific atrocities suffer from a sense of hopelessness, despair and incompetence at not being able to stop such tragedies. Their self esteem is radically diminished because of this. A normal reaction to powerlessness is to regain control. How many of us need to be in control of "Mission"? Why? Many reasons, but I believe a major reason is Trauma. This reaction actually shifts some very basic life principals. The shift is from 'God is in charge' to 'I am in charge, I know Gods' will and I will do it.' Trauma makes us very willful and controlling. Entering into the pain of powerlessness can start to free the Spirit. You see that you have no control over other people, or events. You are powerless. Your vision changes with that insight. This brings you back into "right relationship" with God and others .You take up the proper position in life, God is the Creator, the All powerful one and I am the creature of God. I have no power over anything, but I am not helpless. The person who walks this way has a calling to deep peace instead of driveness of acting as Messiah. It is a call to be able to see what is, it is about knowing your limitations and looking at stark reality in the eye, making new choices. It is about accepting the world for how it is and not how it should be.

STEP 3. Trust and safety.

Further down the traumatized body there are major issues concerning the lack of trust and safety. Trauma destroys the root of safety. Unconsciously the person believes that no one can be trusted. You view others with suspicion, your capacity for intimacy is compromised thus severing the individuals link with their community. This brings further isolation, loneliness and misunderstanding. At this point your view of a loving God changes. From one who believed in god before the traumatic event to one who now questions "How could a loving God allow such a tragedy to happen?" Strangely some people whose faith in God was weak before the event find that their faith in God has increased, seeing that God is larger than the traumatic event in which I survived. Underneath that realization is the fact that in truth I have lost the capacity to trust myself. Sometimes in traumatic situations you realize that you may have, or think you may have made some "bad' decisions. You move out of the wisdom of the body and build large protective walls, learning to live in your head, isolating yourself from yourself and others. How can this be healed? How do you learn again to trust the world? Stage one in healing is learning to trust yourself. Fear of your own poor judgment has to be embraced. Movement into the frozen body needs to take place. A person may have to learn her own thoughts, wants and feelings. People who have been traumatized do not know their own feelings. They have become externally referenced. Reclaiming one's own feelings is extremely frightening. It means that you have to learn to become internally referenced. This journey is like someone who has frostbite. When you are numb you do not feel anything. One of the hardest stages in dealing with frostbite is bringing feeling back into the body, it is extremely painful. Reclaiming trust in your own feelings is that painful journey out of isolation into intimacy with yourself. By doing this you slowly learn to live by the wisdom of the body, reclaiming a whole new relationship with yourself. Having learnt to trust yourself, you can then take down some of the protective walls, allowing you to reach out to contact others. Re contacting the core of your own wisdom, allows you to be intimate with others. This stage moves you from lack of trust and isolation into intimacy.

STEP 4 Shame.

Shame is the experience of being "seen" as deficient, bad and undesirable, it causes an inner sense of being insufficient and diminished as a person. Shame causes blindness. Your eyes are the gateway to your soul. Shame takes your soul away. It binds it in darkness. Shame like evil thrives in darkness. Shame like evil thrives on despair. Shame wounds so profoundly. It is the killer of soul and Spirit. A shame bound person finds it deeply painful to look inward. It is easier to look outward, point fingers and blame. Looking inward feels like "sure death". Healing from shame is like embracing the mystery of "death and Resurrection", "darkness and light". The struggle between "Good and evil" is on! In PTSD therapy, the living truth is what matters. The truth can set you free in mind and body, but the Spirit looks for the truth of the Resurrection. I believe that shame binds you in a despairing black hell. No "theory" can release you from this, only the truth of the resurrection. Only one who has "been there" and risen to "light" can pierce the darkness of another's hell. Only the person in hell can see the spirit of freedom and hope, authentically held out, by one who has journeyed that way. It is essential that therapists have walked their own mystery of death and resurrection before working with trauma victims. Trauma victims are acutely aware of "truth" and are searching for "resurrection". Therapists are called to be "resurrection". Darkness cannot pierce darkness, only light can do that. Clients in turn are called to be resurrected people. In that way "resurrection" spreads. In a 2nd letter from St. Clare of Assisi to Agnes of Prague, St Clare says, "Gaze upon Him."(4)(The Lord) Looking at the word, "gazing", I realize that you cannot gaze if you are bound in shame. Gazing means a long, slow, loving, inward look, not just a detached "head" looking. The call is to gaze at the wounds of Christ. He hangs suspended on the wooden cross gazing back at my wounds. The call is to gaze through the wounds, go into the wounds and allow the wounds to be opened up to the gaze of someone who loves you. This is painful, to allow someone else to look upon you .But, there is an even greater process and that is to gaze lovingly upon your own self and be able to say, "I love myself". Healing from shame is about Resurrection. The question to be asked is, "Am I a resurrected person?" Eyes are damaged by shame. In the Book of Tobit, Tobit's eyes are blinded by hot sparrow's droppings. Doctors could do nothing for him and for four years he remained blind. Likewise shame blinds. The story of Tobits recovery of sight is very profound. Only when the "FISH" medicine is put on the eyes can he see and "look on the light." And he exclaims, "I can see, my son, the light of my eyes." Once we deal with shame, it does restore our sight and we are able to see the "child within" again.

STEP 5. Grief.

Grief can be defined as an intense mental anguish, throwing a person into deep sorrow. One suffers in anguish at seeing a stark reality. Grief is one of the most feared emotions. In grief we appear to "lose control". Grief brings us to tears. You can only cry when you see what you have lost. When you are completely numb, you do not know what you have lost. Grief comes when the iceberg of the unconscious begins to thaw and the waters start to flow. The waters are both "salty and refreshing", both heal. You cannot skip grief. Grieving is about who you have become, it is about grieving your lost potential. In the Book of Lamentation it says, "There is no sorrow like my sorrow". In the 4th letter of St. Clare to Agnes of Prague, she says, "All you who pass by the way, look and see if there is any suffering like my suffering."(5) In grieving from trauma, that is exactly how you feel. You do feel like crying out to anyone who passes by? Look and see! "Is there any suffering like my suffering?" You feel like prostrating at all the sorrows and losses, the lost relationships, the lost potential, the lost possibilities. The journey of grieving and sorrow is a journey into acceptance. Acceptance of who you are now and how trauma has affected you. There is a mixture of joy and sorrow. Joy at the wisdom gained. Sorrow at what might have been.

STEP 6. Emptiness.

There has been so much cleansing and searching and acceptance of the woundedness of life. It has been like a review of your whole life with all its joys and sorrows. Now there is only emptiness. It is "The Cana feast." The old has run out and it is time to wait for something new to be born. There is no time factor to how long to wait, it is another waiting in darkness. Feelings of struggle and pain may disappear, simply leaving you with emptiness and lostness. Where does your life go now? Who are you? When you are stuck in trauma you may have a very strong externalized identity such as, a good worker, a project manager, a great missionary. The journey into trauma has been a journey of purification and transformation, waiting for a new inner identity to emerge. Most certainly I feel that missionaries have a unique opportunity to embrace a new spirituality of trauma. Liberation theology has been imported and seeds sown in Africa. The plants however are weak in many parts of Africa and often short lived. Is this because the underlying issues of trauma and violence have not been addressed? The choked and traumatized Spirit needs healing? I believe that God calls us to wholeness of life. The world today is drastically traumatized. Some people may look for therapy for PTSD and deal with the fractured mind. Some therapies may deal with the traumatized mind and body. This does not go far enough. Violence traumatizes mind, body, soul and spirit. Mind and body must first be united in healing to allow the healed body to be used as an instrument in healing the traumatized soul and Spirit. We are looking these days as missionary groups for the release of the Spirit. I believe the answer is within. Missionary groups are bound in trauma, are bound in the denial of trauma and so will remain the power of our Spirit. In trauma the Trinity of mind, body and soul is fragmented and broken. Release will come when we delve into the "new mission "territory and I believe the Spirit will flow abundantly.

STEP 7. New relationship with God.

In Robert Grants article, "Trauma in Missionary life." he says, "Last but not least, a mission spirituality needs to be developed that is able to find meaning and direction for those constantly faced with violence, oppression and stark expressions of evil and inhumanity. The martyr motive which formally allowed men and women to deal with changes in culture as well as violence is no longer sufficient. Spirituality's grounded in martyrdom only encourage people to internalize trauma and its' destructive effects instead of working through the trauma." (6.) I believe that God is at the center of our lives waiting on us to come to Him as "Bride". The Bride is not one who is languishing among the flowers, but the bride has the same destiny as the bridegroom. The way of trauma takes us to that place. We are called out of isolation, into intimacy, from being bound in shame to being known as friend. Imagine a world where people dealt with trauma. Imagine peace, dialogue, intimacy. My journey through trauma has been a long journey. I never imagined that pain could be so painful. Yet that wound has now turned into a great blessing. I have the realization that life is a mixture of good and evil. That life will never be a utopia. It will always be the struggle of the pilgrim way. That realization is the joy of life. This leaves me with one thing I believe in and one thing I know and that is that evil will never triumph if we keep our hearts open to love and that I don't believe in endings only knew beginnings. I know I have a new beginning in my life with Matthew and this chapter has yet to be written.

An Appendix For Missionaries

Some time ago I wrote an article called "The Spirituality of Trauma". Since that time our world has changed forever. Trauma has been staged dramatically in nearly every continent. Sadly I did not see world leaders, spiritual or political, effectively rise up to face the challenge of healing the wounded soul of all those whose lives have been radically touched, damaged and wounded by these traumatic events. I do know that traumatic wounds need to be healed by some one who knows "Hell". This is why I feel that we have not faced the challenge offered to us as Christian people to go to hell, to become the wounded healers that the world is groaning for.

MISSIONARY GROUPS LIVING WITH TRAUMA

At present many missionary groups are facing crisis in numbers, vocations, leadership, vision and viability. Congregations are heroically "slogging on". Younger members are not following the designated pattern of the good missionary. In fact there seems to be a disintegration. Splits are occurring and people are looking back over their shoulders and saying, "at least in the old days we knew what we were doing and where we were going." Confusion abounds; stress, anxiety and overload are occurring. Fewer people are doing more work and in all of that we are looking for the "Magical Cure" that someone, somewhere, will get a spark of "new Vision" and order back into our lives. This will not happen unless we are prepared to stop, literally, from the frenzy of our lives and ministry. Many groups have "let go" of external structures while maintaining a rigid interior structure. Time has come for the Inner Journey. New structures need to be put in place to start this inner journey. This needs to be addressed seriously. Trauma and PTSD are central issues affecting our humanity, yet the topic is ignored and put on the "back burner" for another day. I believe that if missionary groups embraced the reality of trauma and PTSD in their congregations and lives then the magical cure may be dawning. Few are willing to take the risk, invest the money, time, confusion and effort. I believe, in dealing with the effects of violence found in missionary congregations, we would find our humanity and become more grounded. We could live our limitations and find the compassion of the poverty of both the Incarnation and the Crucifixion. This would lead to intimacy, spirituality, joy, vitality and, in all that, find a new mission for the Church serving the broken traumatized body. People would find meaning in this vision. There is hope for the future. Education is needed on violence, trauma and war. People need to be trained to help missionaries in violent situations. Missionaries need debriefing when they go home and centers need to be set up for those suffering from PTSD. Mission societies have to change with the signs of the times, if not, then we will be a traumatized missionary body serving a traumatized Church in Africa. This issue needs to be addressed not just by individuals, but by missionary unions. We are called to change, not in order to survive but to reflect fullness of life. We are called to be resurrected, light bringers, we do that by descending into hell, sitting in the darkness and rising to new life, and a new missionary era.

THE WOUNDING

Trauma is an overpowering experience, which wounds us spiritually and psychologically. It removes us from a world known and secure, to the devastation of not knowing and being left with the question "Why?" With this in mind I have often reflected on the book of Genesis where it says, "Yahweh God caused to spring up from the soil every kind of tree, enticing to look at and good to eat, with the tree of life and the tree of knowledge of good and evil in the middle of the garden." Then Yahweh God gave the man this admonition, "You may eat in deed of all the trees in the garden. Nevertheless, of the tree of the knowledge of good and evil you are not to eat, for on the day you eat of it you shall most surely die." The two trees in the middle of the garden are sacred and Adam and Eve are admonished not to eat of the fruit of the knowledge of good and evil. Why? This is a very good question. "WHY" is the question asked after most atrocities. Usually there is no answer. Here again I ask Why? Why can we mere mortals with a thirst for all things not be allowed to touch that tree. Surely that is an enticement for some people? Surely if we touched that tree we would know things beyond mere mortal hood. In the Admonitions of St Francis it says, "What you are before God, you are that and nothing more." And what we are before God is simply that we are merely mortal and no more. Knowledge of the tree of good and evil is in the realm of the Gods of Light and Darkness. To touch that is to burn. The power of that knowledge would be too much for us to contain. We have great liberties given to us, but warned not to dabbled in the realm of the Deities. My next question then is all important. What happens when the tree of evil steps out and touches us? I can list some of the recent atrocities of beheadings, and suicide bombings as the tree of evil affecting our world today. I ask again, what happens to our soul when the tree of evil steps out and touches us? We have been admonished "not to touch" by God, but a touch is a touch, no matter who does the touching. Is this a malaise of the world today, has much of our world been touched by the tree of evil and our church stands impotent with finding the antidote. Today there is a lot of vicious trauma. The tree of evil is actively stepping out. In my experience, I have realised that there are four main roads taken once that touch has been extended. They are,

1)

The person is consumed with pain. This pain ignites and festers into bitterness and hatred. The person is engorged over time with this, they change, they become focused on their pain with notions of revenge. Eventually if the climate is ripe and there is no community response to that persons wound, you find that hatred begets hatred. The person is so consumed by the event and is not able to enter the call in their wound, that they eventually reach out in hatred and beget more trauma onto someone else as a way of venting their compacted grief. This is their way of pain relief and they have passed on their wound.

The next scenario is 2)

The person is consumed with pain. They continuously ask "Why"
There seems to be no answer or end to this.

To ask "why" is to try and understand evil. This is too much for
any soul to hold. No one can understand the full power of evil or the
full power of good. This is why we are originally asked not to touch
the trees in the middle of the garden. By trying to understand the
"why" of an atrocity can cause us to burn. Eventually, continually
asking that question can consume the person so much that they
become depressed and depression turns to anguish and deepest
darkness. If there is no one there to help hold their pain or acknowledge
their suffering, then an option for that person is suicide. This is their
way to end the pain. They have passed on their trauma.

The next scenario is 3)

The person is consumed with pain. It is so bad that they cut
themselves off from any feeling. They "numb out", as to live with
that level of anguish would lead to suicide. The person becomes
addicted to many things as a means of controlling their pain. Their
life may become unmanageable and out of control, but through
addictions they have pacified the all-consuming grief and embodied
their trauma.

I believe low-grade depression, grief and addictive behaviour
are serious consequences of trauma lived out in missionary
organisations.

The fourth option is "The Eye of God" This takes you to Holy
Saturday, the place of transformation.

THE FOURTH ROAD

We will take a look at the forth option. So many people fall into
the first three categories, there seems to be no map made out to
move through the anguish of healing, but to look at the "eye of God"
may help. To do this we have to look at Good Friday. I believe we

163

are a Good Friday people, I believe too that this is where some of our trouble lies. We can carry the cross, walk the walk, dig our heels in and suffer as good as the next person. We look to Christ for inspiration and imitation. He carried the cross to the end and suffered in doing so. We in imitation do the same. This is where I feel we have to learn the difference between "change" and "transformation". Imitating the way of the cross in this way may bring about change, usually it calls for us to start all over again with a new project, a new cross, new people to live with, but with the same pattern adopted. There has been no transformative change in us. Why? I believe because we are good, Good Friday people. We walk Holy Thursday, Good Friday and then jump over to the Resurrection. Something is missing in this scenario. The transformative moment is the call to Saturday. How do we get there and what is its meaning?

GOOD FRIDAY

Good Friday was a day of torture and cruelty beyond understanding. It is known as the day Christ died. I look at Good Friday as Gods day of helpless anguish. I believe it is this God of the Trinity whom we are called to imitate. Can you imagine having all the available power of the universe at your fingertips? Can you imagine watching your child being tortured and brutally murdered? Can you imagine knowing that your intervention could stop this, but literally for the love of the human race you have to stand by and watch this atrocity? How on earth was God feeling at that moment? I believe that Good Friday is God's day of Suffering. We zoom in on our lady standing at the foot of the cross helplessly watching, but she had no power whatsoever to stop this. God had all the power of the universe to stop it, why did he not. He did not stop the murder, so as to allow all of us from here on in to know that we are not alone. Gods choice was to be powerless and choose us over his son. What agony, what anguish, what love and mercy. His utter powerlessness transformed darkness forever. He allowed His Son to give us a map for Transformative union and redemption. God's power in the face of evil would have left us all in darkness and with no road maps to live by. Powerlessness in Gods case led to life and light. First of all, though, His son had to die and go to hell. This too is where we are called to go to if our suffering is to be redeemed.

HOLY SATURDAY

What do we do on Holy Saturday? Most people don't do anything. We clean, pick daffodils, go shopping for a leg of lamb and Easter eggs while the central day passes unnoticed. Holy Saturday is about Christ's descent into hell, to darkness and a raw black, bleak place of blood, sweat and tears. It is a place of utter disillusionment and grief, a place of felt abandonment where there is nothing. It is a place of complete isolation and detachment. A central issue in this raw place is grief. We will do anything rather than go to that anguished place. I believe trauma is passed on by people trying to bypass this grief. We will hate, lash out, use addictions to avoid going to that place. Grief is total surrender. We either survive it and become transformed or we don't. Christ went there so from that moment we would all, in our darkest moment, know we were not alone. Healing is passed on by people who have survived this place.

THE RESURRECTION

We know nothing about Christ's descent into hell; all we do know is that in resurrection, nobody recognised him. Jn 20 v11-17, Mary, the woman who loved him most and had watched him die did not recognise him till He said her name. Luke 24 V 13-35 There was something preventing them on the road to Emmaus from recognising Christ. He was not just changed but transformed. Jn 21 V1-14. I find this a very wonderful description of resurrection and trauma recovery. Once again, the disciples who loved Him did not recognise him, yet they followed his instructions to throw the nets in a different place. Only when they heard his voice did Simon know it was "He". He wanted to share a meal of grilled fish and bread. I find this interesting that they did not recognise him and like an invalid He could only eat grilled fish. This part of the Gospel always reminds me how fragile resurrection and trauma recovery is. We think that it is full of power, but resurrection scenes are full of fragility, healing and a grounded sense of knowing who we are. There is an alleluia but I believe the manifestation of that power comes with Pentecost. Many times we mix the two up. We are called to live and find meaning in this new fragile state and called to engage the world in resurrection as lover, bride, priest. Recovery is long and hard. It involves living within our newfound limitations and resurrected vulnerability but brings with it a wisdom that only one who has been touched by the central tree knows. Different spiritualities may help to take us along this path. One only has to look at:

St Francis of Assisi

St Catherine of Sienna

St John of the Cross

St Ignatius Loyola

St Clare of Assisi

All these saints have a history of trauma and displacement. If you look at most of the lives of the Saints, you will find a history of Trauma and if you look at the lives of missionaries today you will also see a history of trauma.

THE CALL

The difference today is that missionaries are not encouraged to walk the way of their wound. Walking the way of their wound is a way of life, not just a short renewal moment supposed to "fix" you and get you back in the saddle. Walking the way of wounded ness is about Transformation, not just change. It is about entering the wound and listening to what the darkness of the wound is calling from you. There is a definite calling, moving you into the wisdom of what it means to be fully human. This call can mean discovery of fragility and limitation. The paschal mystery seems to descend, Holy Saturday becomes the dark mantle enmeshed with darkness itself. This is the time of life or death, freedom or binding. It is an acute moment of either continuing the same patterns or radically transforming your whole being.

Walking the healing path is living the paschal mystery. There are some people who have walked this journey. They have been in hell and risen. When I was in a therapy centre in MA USA I was dealing with a traumatic memory of witnessing two men being murdered in Uganda. I had arrived at a place where I felt I had reached darkness in its most "utter" form. I felt no one could reach me. It was then that I had a very intense interaction with my therapist were she verbally slapped me into hearing that she too had been in hell. I recall just staring at her eyes, looking for the truth of her statement, looking for hell. What I found was light and a new path out of hell. Strangely, in my darkest moment I found Light. I realised most acutely the truth in what she had said to me about hell and would have sensed if she had been lying .At that moment I needed her to be telling the truth. In fact I needed the truth of hell to be real and I thank God every day that my therapist had walked the way of her wound to its end and that her wound took her to hell. I realised the necessity of hell and people going there, I realised for myself if I wanted to be in the healing ministry I too needed to go to hell. I realised the healthiness of going to hell and the foolishness of pretending I was whole. Being whole would never have saved me, being wounded did I realised too, that this is the difference between Good Friday and Holy Saturday.

It was appalling for me now to see how people ignored their wounds, trivialised their wounds and denied them allowing the illusion of wholeness to prevail. Wholesomeness can occur by entering the wound, descending and rising. The world is crying out for people who have transformed their pain into wisdom and who have transformed the senselessness of trauma into meaning. If we ignore the wound, we ignore the "calling" that trauma asks of us.

If we take trauma seriously, we take our spirituality to a different dimension were the adult Christ is being called out of us.

This spiritual pathway brings us to a oneness firstly with our self. Trauma fragments and destroys, recovery brings union and restores hope. This may feel like walking in a strange land for those who have been traumatised because they have been alienated from themselves for a long time. This is the evil of trauma. It alienates and isolates, it destroys the potential for intimacy with self, others and God. When that intimacy is destroyed then the potential for evil is unlimited.

The meaning of life is to find meaning. Trauma has the ability to irreversibly change a persons life and if that person is to live well, then she has to make meaning for herself out of it. To have meaning means that I am in union, firstly with myself then others. It is about being in intimate relationship. Being intimate with someone calls you to be vulnerable and revelatory. It is about feeling so safe with someone that it is OK to be wounded. So much time is wasted in pretending to have no wounds, but relationship allows these wounds to be explored and loved.

When that occurs there is union and the fruits of that are joy, peace, love, trust and hope. This is an actual state of being, a Pentecost which trauma recovery can bring about.

My hope for the missionary church is that we hear the call of the wound, enter the wound, walk the way of the wound and allow the wound to transform our lives becoming vital, alive and filled with the spirit of Pentecost.

HEART OF GOLD

Tynecastle legend's daughter helps the sick in Africa

By BRUCE BLAIR

EXCLUSIVE

A SCOTS angel – daughter of a football legend – is in the front line of the fight against famine in Ethiopia.

Caring nun Sister Jo Wardhaugh, an Edinburgh-trained nurse, has spent the past three years tending the sick with her mobile clinic.

Angel of mercy Sister Jo comforts one of her young patients in famine-ravaged Ethiopia

Hearts great Jimmy Wardhaugh

Sister Jo's health battle

GOOD health is something we all take for granted, but for a Scottish nun working in Ethiopia, it's literally a matter of life and death, writes Sean McGuigan.

Sister Jo Wardhaugh, of the Franciscan Missionary Sisters for Africa, has returned to Scotland to take her final vows after spending three years working in the Gamu Goffe region of Ethiopia, where she came face to face with disease and famine.

Sister Jo, who hails from Edinburgh, trained as a nurse before entering the order, and her medical knowledge is well needed in the area where pneumonia and children born under the poorest weight are common.

The main thrust of the order's work is a health education programme and lessons for the women in midwifery.

Training is given for the women in how to deliver as well as care for the babies properly and a good caring and clean spirit can be fostered among them.

Such basics as clean water are provided by means of a hand-dug well.

The situation in the region is not helped by the civil war in the country which leaves many women and children the victims of famine and drought.

Gamu Goffe may be 700 kilometres from the war region, but this does not mean the problems are any less.

In fact, before Sister Jo returned to Scotland she was waging a twin battle against meningitis and famine.

"The people are helped by the mobile clinic which tours the region," says Sister Jo.

"The aim of the clinic is to reduce disease by promoting health and cleanliness."

Sister Jo's interest in this particular vocation was stimulated by the "bravery of the sisters I met in Uganda while working out there as a lay missionary.

"Their courage in the face of danger was inspiring," she said.

"I felt moved to serve the poor, they have such a wonderful spirit about them, despite the difficulties they face."

Sister Jo has a sister who is a nun in the order of the Society of the Sacred Heart

and her father was the famous Hearts goalscorer Jimmy Wardhaugh.

Sister Jo (left) feeds to an Ethiopian man and her baby who had visited her mobile clinic in Gamu Goffe.

Taking a rest from healing

by RICHARD NEVILLE

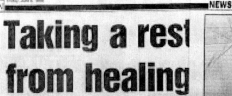

LOVELY RAIN: After Ethiopia, Jo Wardhaugh finds the Edinburgh rain a treat

Sisters

Papers

Rest for nun daughter of Hearts hero

Famine fighter returning home

RICHARD NEVILLE

THE DAUGHTER of an Edinburgh football hero, who is one of a group of nuns dedicated to fighting famine in Ethiopia, is coming home next month for a well-earned rest.

Sister Jo Wardhaugh (33) has used her skills as a nurse to treat the sick in the often treacherous conditions of the Ethiopian mountains for the past three years.

Now the Edinburgh trained nurse is coming home for a three-month break to be with her family.

Her mother Jean, widow of Hearts great Scotland striker Jimmy Wardhaugh, who died 13 years ago aged 49, spoke today of her daughter's courageous work.

She said: "They see a awful lot of disease and malnutrition in the villages, but the work they do is important and helps a lot of people.

They do normal medical work as well as studies and child health care and ante-

natal clinics — they are trying to educate the people about the benefits of healthy living and cleanliness.

"I can't worry for her all the time, but I am always conscious of her being there."

Mrs Wardhaugh, of Windmill Place, Edinburgh, spent five weeks in the Kena Goffe region, south of the civil war area of Eritrea, with Jo during Christmas 1988 and now by herself the work being done with the poor and the sick by the sisters of the Franciscan Missionaries for Africa.

She added: "It was a wonderful experience being in such a beautiful country and the people are lovely.

"The sisters work about 10,000 feet up in the mountains so they don't have a great deal of home comforts, but I was glad to see for myself the work they are doing."

Jo will spend three months back in Scotland when she will take her final vows and then return to the fight against famine in Africa.

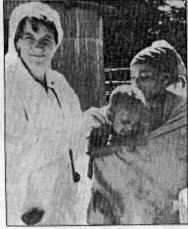

JO WARDHAUGH at work in Ethiopia.

BIBLIOGRAPHY

John Of The Cross For Today: The Dark Night. By Susan Muto.
Quotations From The Jerusalem Bible.
Trauma And Recovery by Judith Herman.
The Way of The Wound by Robert Grant.
Trauma in Missionary Life by Robert Grant.(Article)
Quotations From the Letters of St Clare to Agnes of Prague.From Clare of Assisi Early Documents.
The Writings of Francis. From The Franciscan Omnibus.
The Spirituality of Trauma revised article. First published in 2000 by Human Development Magazine U.S.A.
Stanza 32 The spiritual Canticle. John of the Cross selected writings.

NEWSPAPERS

Scottish Catholic Observer
Daily Record
Edinburgh Evening News